Distinctive
Limoges
Porcelain

Objets d'Art, Boxes and Dinnerware

Keith & Thomas Waterbrook-Clyde

Schiffer Publishing Ltd ®

4880 Lower Valley Road, Atglen, PA 19310 USA

Dedication

To our Friends and Acquaintances Who Have Made Collecting Fun: Yasu, Shirley, Nora, Laurence, Roy, Richard, Raymonde, Jackie, and Beth and Ted.

Designed by John P. Cheek
Type set in Zaph Chancery Bd BT/
Souvenir Lt BT/Humanist 521 BT

ISBN: 0-7643-1260-X
Printed in China
1 2 3 4

Published by Schiffer Publishing Ltd.
4880 Lower Valley Road
Atglen, PA 19310
Phone: (610) 593-1777; Fax: (610) 593-2002
E-mail: Schifferbk@aol.com
Please visit our web site catalog at
www.schifferbooks.com
We are always looking for people to write books on new and related subjects. If you have an idea for a book please contact us at the above address.

This book may be purchased from the publisher.
Include $3.95 for shipping.
Please try your bookstore first.
You may write for a free catalog.

In Europe, Schiffer books are distributed by
Bushwood Books
6 Marksbury Ave.
Kew Gardens
Surrey TW9 4JF England
Phone: 44 (0)208 392-8585
Fax: 44 (0)208 392-9876
E-mail: Bushwd@aol.com
Free postage in the UK. Europe: air mail at cost

Values

The values in this book are intended as only a guide for collectors, since prices for older Limoges porcelain and contemporary Limoges boxes vary significantly by region, by country and by what's popular at a particular moment in time. Auctions on the Internet, especially on eBay, have moderated to some extent the variations in values in different regions and countries; however, there are still swings in the popularity of particular kinds of pieces and their corresponding values over a period in time. In assigning values, we have taken the perspective of the knowledgeable Limoges collector, taking into account among other things the design and shapes of the blanks, decorating styles and themes, and specific manufacturers and decorators. For example, the vase decorated by S. Mounier, which is on the cover, is an important historical piece. During the 1850s, Mounier was a highly recognized decorator whose work was exhibited at the Exposition Universelle of 1855 in Anvers, France; yet very few pieces of his work have survived. Only advanced collectors of Limoges porcelain would recognize the importance and rarity of this kind of piece. Finally, there are many pieces that are "cross" collectibles, and we have tried to take this into account as well. For example, a Limoges powder jar or a Robj porcelain piece may have a certain value for Limoges collectors, yet a different—and often higher—value for collectors of powder jars or Robj pieces.

Contents

Acknowledgments

Once again we have leaned on our good friend, Yasumasa Tanano, to not only help us with the marks but also to provide us with many pieces to photograph from his collection. He is also our counselor—he is available to listen to our ideas and provide us with advice. Roy Betancourt took off the better part of a day to let us photograph many of his Haviland pieces. Jacqueline and Marv Lowensteiner have once again come through and provided us with many photographs from their very fine Limoges porcelain collection. Beth and Ted Bodenschatz and Richard Rendall also sent us numerous photographs. We have also learned a lot from Shirley Dickerson, the president of S&D Limoges. Many of her Limoges boxes she had designed from silver and other pieces in her own personal collection. Laurence de La Grange, manager of Le Tallec, has been very helpful in providing us information about the Le Tallec studio and in answering our many questions. Claude Souffron, who is the manager of the workshop and who has been with Le Tallec for nearly 40 years, identified the names and dates of the different Le Tallec patterns. Margaret Wilmerding from Artoria, Richard Sonking from Rochard, and Michael Perera and Patrick Kelso from Dubarry sent us many of their boxes so that we could photograph them and include them in this book. Leny Davidson from Chamart and Atilda Alvarido from Limoges Collectors Society sent us photographs and transparencies. Many thanks also to George Gati and Raymonde Limoges who willingly translated many French passages for us.

Introduction

In our first book on Limoges porcelain, *The Decorative Art of Limoges Porcelain and Boxes* (Schiffer Publishing, 1999), we provided introductory information on old Limoges porcelain and contemporary boxes, and included an historical overview of porcelain making in Limoges. We also provided photographs that represented a wide range of old Limoges porcelain and contemporary boxes. In this volume, we are not going to repeat any of the background information that was in the first book; instead we are going to provide considerably more information about the individual pieces that we have photographed for this book. As a result, the captions that accompany the photographs have been greatly expanded.

In this book we have for the most part concentrated on pieces that, by our definition, are *distinctive*. We have defined *distinctive* broadly to include the following: 1) pieces that are well decorated or not decorated at all, 2) pieces that are representative of the works of well known Limoges artists, 3) pieces that represent specific decorating techniques and styles, 4) pieces that represent unusual and/or beautiful blanks, 5) pieces that are atypical and/or rare, and 6) pieces of historical significance. Of course, many of these categories overlap. In the majority of the captions that accompany the photographs, we will explain why the pieces are *distinctive*, or in a few cases *not distinctive*, and by extension why we have included them in this volume. We have tried, on the other hand, to strike a balance between pieces that are too unique or scarce and those that the average collector might be expected to encounter. We want this book to be useful, in the everyday sense, to the collector. It is not a book for the museum curator, except for the section on Marks.

In a real sense, this book is also about the kinds of pieces that interest us personally as collectors—it reflects our tastes, what we like and don't like, and our opinions about what is *distinctive* and *not distinctive*. This volume is not intended, in other words, to be a history of porcelain with a sampling of representative pieces along the way. It is more like a personal guided tour. For example, we have included a relatively large number of Sandoz pieces, because we personally like his designs, and a few Art Deco pieces commissioned by Robj, the Paris retailer, in business from 1921-1931. We have also included a disproportionate number of cake plates and cups and saucers. The cake plates, in particular, illustrate some of the very early decorating styles and tastes beginning in the 1860s. The cups and saucers provide a wide variety of different porcelain blanks and patterns as well as decorating styles and methods throughout the last 150 years.

Furthermore, this volume also shows our growing appreciation of the beauty of many undecorated white blanks. Some of these pieces, of course, were not intended for decoration, while others just never reached the decorating workshop. In many cases the blanks themselves are works of art, and we are happy some of them were never decorated. Often, the decorators—whether professional or amateur, French or American—gave little attention to the intricate patterns on many of the blanks during the decorating process. There were, of course, exceptions: both Pairpoint, a Massachusetts based decorating studio in the late 1800s, which apparently had a decorating studio in Limoges, and Ovington Brothers, a retailer based in New York, which also decorated porcelain and was in business from c. 1870s through the first part of the 20th century, carefully considered the pattern in the porcelain as part of the decorating process. The major decorating companies in Limoges sometimes followed this practice as well, especially when decorating some of their high-end pieces.

We have also included pieces decorated by some of the well-known artists in Limoges. Unlike other sources on Limoges porcelain, we have given considerable attention to pieces decorated by Atelier Le Tallec in Paris. All Le Tallec pieces are exquisitely hand painted on Limoges porcelain, and their work represents some of the finest porcelain decoration in the world. But their pieces are pricey. In addition to dinnerware and giftware, Le Tallec decorates many traditionally shaped boxes—rectangles, squares, ovals and heart and egged shaped pieces.

Finally, just a few words about Limoges porcelain in general. Limoges refers to a region in France, where kaolin and feldspar, the key ingredients of hard past porcelain, were discovered around 1764. The Limoges region is located about 200 miles southwest of Paris. The first piece of Limoges porcelain dates from 1771.

Throughout the years there were many companies that produced and decorated porcelain in Limoges. Some of the better known companies include Haviland & Co., Théodore Haviland, Pouyat, Guérin, Raynaud and Bernardaud. Most of the manufactures of porcelain also decorated porcelain as well as sold blanks (undecorated white ware) to other decorating companies and the general public around the world. Porcelain that is also decorated in Limoges usually has an underglaze green mark, which identifies the manufacturer, and an overglaze mark, which identifies the decorating company. There have been many Limoges companies over the last 230 years. Looking through the section on marks will provide the reader with a good idea of the number of companies that have manufactured and decorated Limoges porcelain throughout the years.

Limoges Boxes

In terms of "subject" boxes—boxes which we defined in our first volume on Limoges porcelain as ones that are shaped to represent a specific subject, like a dog, fish, etc.—we have chosen to include pieces from the major companies that import boxes in the U.S. We know that pieces from these companies were decorated in Limoges, and the overall quality of the decorator is usually very good. These companies include Artoria (a manufacturer, decorator and exporter), and the import companies S&D Limoges, Chamart, Rochard, and Dubarry. All of these companies mark their boxes, although S&D Limoges only began marking their boxes in 1999 and only marks those boxes that are decorated exclusively for them. While most of these companies have their own decorators in Limoges, they also import boxes from major Limoges decorating studios, like Parry Vieille.

Although the contemporary Limoges boxes first began appearing in the U.S. in the 1960s, it was not until the 1980s that they became a popular collectible. Today, with the increasing reach of the Internet, Limoges boxes of every variety are available everywhere. The quality of the decoration varies from very poor to veritable *objets d'art*. It is important for the collector to understand all of the variations of Limoges boxes that are currently on the market.

First, many boxes are being sold as "Limoges like" boxes or "Limoges style" boxes. The porcelain for these boxes was clearly not made in Limoges, as usually indicated by the company markings on the bottom of the boxes. Many of these boxes are made in the U.S. while a great number of others are made in Asia. Additionally, many boxes are now appearing with "fake" Limoges marks. These marks include the word *Limoges* but not the word *France*. (See the photographs of these marks in the *Mark Section*.) Nearly all of these boxes are made in Asia. As this book goes to press, it is certain that additional "fake" Limoges marks will begin appearing on the market. It is important that the country of origin, France, be part of the company mark on the bottom of the box.

Many French companies are also beginning to "dump" their "seconds" on the market as well. These pieces do not usually carry the mark of the Limoges decorating studio on the box. This phenomenon is occurring with increasing frequency. Porcelain manufacturing companies, of course, are also selling their blanks (undecorated boxes) all over the world, something that they have done since the beginning of the manufacturing of porcelain. The majority of these boxes are decorated by amateur decorators and the quality is usually, although not always, very poor. Finally, there are a number of very poor decorators in Limoges that are decorating boxes as well.

Many of the markings on Limoges boxes can also be deceiving. A box is often inscribed with a number to give the indication that it is part of a limited edition. The edition may be limited, but it is only limited by the number of boxes that can be sold. Some companies also try to convey exclusivity and value solely by providing the size of the edition, e.g., 31/500. Unfortunately, in these cases the quality of decoration of the box is extremely poor, so that potentially 500 poorly decorated boxes will be sold.

Furthermore, a "limited edition" only means that a particular decorating design is limited, not the porcelain blank (shape). Hundreds of more boxes will be distributed with the same shape but decorated in different colors and styles. In fact, a cat, for example, may become a dog, on the same blank, depending on the decoration. Many boxes will also be marked with the initials of the decorator. This is rather meaningless, since it is impossible to identify the artist and thus to look for pieces decorated by a particular individual. (The case of Le Tallec is somewhat different. Le Tallec, for example, never identifies the full name of the artist, since each piece has to be "hand painted with the same painstaking methods of [Camille] Le Tallec." This is called "la main Le Tallec." – From a personal letter dated 9 December 1999 from Laurence de La Grange, manager of Le Tallec, to the authors.) Some companies, though, are now importing boxes that are marked with the name of the decorator, and this will be helpful to the serious collector in the long run.

Also, don't be fooled by the color of the hardware. The brightness of the hardware is primarily attributed to the amount of acid used in the finishing. Dull or black hardware is not an indication of age. The brass hardware may be bright gold, brown or black, or variations in between. What is important is that the hardware fit snugly and line up when the box is closed.

The method of decoration also varies. Some boxes are totally hand painted, others are decorated with transfers and still others are decorated with a combination of hand painting and transfers. All other things being equal, totally hand painted boxes will hold their value better. Some of the low end boxes are actually decorated by Limoges companies. Limoges Castel, for example, produces almost exclusively boxes that are decorated with transfers. These pieces are easy to identify, since they all have a blue background with usually gold scenes with figures. Fontanille & Marraud, another Limoges company, decorates a majority of their boxes with primarily transfers that have enameled highlights.

The serious Limoges box collector will want to consider several factors. First and foremost is the quality of decoration. The experienced collector will be able to determine the overall quality of the decoration rather easily, based upon personal experience. Secondly, totally hand painted pieces are for the most part more valuable. Next, the application of the brass hardware needs to be well fitted to the porcelain and aligned. Finally, Limoges porcelain boxes that are also decorated in Limoges, or elsewhere in France, will have more value and the decorating mark will include the word *France*.

Since contemporary boxes date, at the earliest, from the 1960s, the age of a box is not yet an important factor in determining value. Also, it is not possible yet to identify the age of a particular box from the mark of the company. (The exception is Le Tallec, which started marking a code for the production date beginning in 1941.) Rochard, for example, uses many different renderings of the name, *Rochard*, for its marks. Simply, different Limoges decorators use different Rochard marks. Also, many boxes imported by S&D Limoges do not even carry the *S&D* mark.

What's important to understand is that the major distributors of Limoges boxes in the U.S. contract with different decorators or studios in Limoges to decorate boxes for them. Fortunately, these companies contract with the best decorators to decorate their boxes, sometimes on an exclusive basis and, at times, only certain decorations are exclusive. All of these companies also import boxes decorated by Parry Vieille, which also carry the Parry Vieille mark.

In many cases, the companies often direct the shape and decoration of the boxes which they import. Artoria, on the other hand, manufactures the porcelain blanks, employs the decorators, exports, and distributes their boxes. All of the boxes from these companies, with the exception of S&D, mark their boxes, which indicates that the boxes are usually well decorated, must meet certain standards and that the boxes were decorated in Limoges. All boxes marked *S&D, Artoria,* and *Chamart* are entirely hand painted. Additionally, the *S&D* mark is used only when the boxes were exclusively designed for S&D Limoges. Artoria also sells porcelain blanks, which are decorated and sold by other companies. Some upscale retailers also work closely with these companies in designing boxes exclusively for them, although this is usually limited to the decorating scheme and not to the porcelain blank. Gump's in San Francisco and Lucy Zahran in Beverly Hills, California, are two such retailers.

Finally, the prices for Limoges boxes vary widely. The values that we have listed for the Limoges boxes from the major companies are the suggested retail prices. It is not uncommon to see these prices discounted by up to 20 percent, or sometime even 30 percent, by smaller retailers and retailers who sell from web sites. The secondary market values for these same pieces are usually 30 percent to 40 percent less than the retail prices as of this writing. Lesser quality boxes, of course, usually sell for substantially less.

Limoges Porcelain

We have organized these photographs into eight major groupings. The first two, Limoges Vases and Limoges Chargers and Plaques, are strictly decorative pieces. While many of the Limoges plates in the third section are also decorative, there are many that were also part of dinnerware sets. Limoges table pieces, coffee and tea service, and cups and saucers—the fourth, fifth and sixth sections, respectively—are, of course, dinnerware pieces. In the seventh section, Limoges specialty pieces, we take a break from all of the dinnerware items and focus on more unusual Limoges pieces, some just decorative and others with more practical purposes. Finally, the last section is devoted to undecorated blanks, which as a group have been under appreciated by collectors.

Limoges Vases

Kerchief Vase, 8.25" high x 4.5" x 3.75", Pouyat porcelain mark 3, c. 1876-1890, and Pouyat decorating mark 4 in red, c. 1876-1890. This is an unusual blank. It appears that this blank was made specifically for this particular decorating theme. The blank, which is not square at the corners or on the sides, looks like a piece of material that has been twisted and tied into knots at the four feet and the four top corners. The front pink panel is a stitched on patch, with two raised corners that have become loose. $500-$600

Fish Vase, 6.5" high, Pouyat porcelain mark 3 in green, c. 1876-1890. Although this vase does not have a decorating mark, this piece was certainly factory decorated. The blank is rare, and the decoration is superb and very detailed. $500+

Terra Cotta Vase, 18" high, Haviland & Co. mark V, 1875-1882. This is an unusually tall Haviland & Co. earthenware vase. The decorating style of this vase reflects the influence of the Japanese decorative arts, which was common during this period. $1,500-$1,800

Pair of Vases, 11" high, T. Haviland decorating mark j in red, c. 1892. These vases have the first T. Haviland decorating mark, and the decoration shows the Japanese influence (*Japonisme*) on the European decorative arts in the last half of the 19th century. The pair is nicely decorated. Pair, $1,200+

Figurine Vase, 17.5" high, Mounier decorating mark 1 in red, c. 1850s. Jean d'Albis (see Bibliography) mentions Mounier as a decorator for Valin et Berthoud, and a piece decorated by Mounier was shown at the 1855 Paris Exposition. (Michael Aaron & Valin jointly operated porcelain factories in Limoges from 1832-1845. Michel Aaron left the firm in 1845, and Valin ran the factories himself, until 1855 when he was joined by his son and son-in-law, Berthoud.) The applied figurine is bisque, with no enamel, and is very detailed. Mounier's choice to leave the figurine in bisque contributes to the overall gossamer effect of the woman figure. This is a very rare piece. $10,000+

Description of the Mounier decorated vase in the Musée National Adrien Dubouché in Limoges. The entry states that the piece was manufactured by Valin, 1855. It is made of three parts and is 1.5 meters high x 0.65 meters in length. The piece came from Mme. Valin, who was associated with Pastaud in Limoges. It was acquired on January 31, 1984 for 50,000 FF.

11

Swan Handled Vase, 12.75" high, Le Tallec decorating mark 3 and φ, 1977, with artist, *JN*. The name of the pattern is *Oiseaux Polychrôme Fond Bleu Décor Coeur*. The raised gold work and the swan handles make this a stunning vase. $1,200+

Blue Vase, 9.5" high, Pouyat porcelain mark 3, c. 1876-1890, and Pouyat decorating mark 4 in red, c. 1876-1890. Pieces with the older Pouyat decorating mark are highly collectible. This vase, with a blue textured background, a very ornate handle, and gold layered fern leaves, is extremely well decorated. This same blank, but decorated differently with thistles, is pictured in the book on the exposition of Pouyat's work (see Meslin-Perrier in Bibliography). This vase in different styles was originally listed in a catalogue under the heading, *Japonaise*. $400-$500

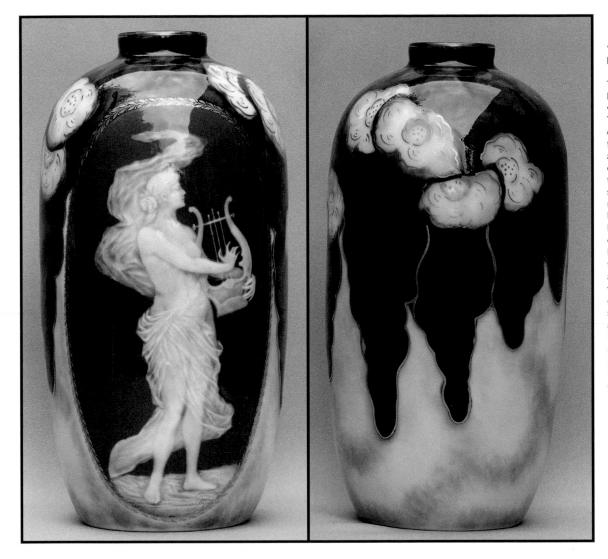

"Terra Cotta"/Relief Vase, 10" high, Tharaud porcelain mark 1 impressed, 1920-1945, and Tharaud decorating mark 2 in blue, 1920-1945. This vase, which is porcelain, represents Tharaud's pioneering experimentation with high firing temperatures, glazes, and deep shades of blue, gray, emerald green, and lilac. Note that there are two decorating styles on this vase—a figure in relief and the subtle distinct but "harmonious" colors that have the appearance of terra cotta. Tharaud made two kinds of products: vases like this one which were for the art "connoisseurs" and others which were made in large quantities to sell in the regular stores. Sadly, Tharaud's pieces are under appreciated in the U.S. market; however, they represent some of the finest porcelain decoration in Limoges in the early 20th century. $450+

"Terra Cotta" Vase, 7" high and 7.25" in diameter, Tharaud mark 1.1 in green, 1920-1945, and Tharaud decorating mark 2 in blue, 1920-1945. This porcelain vase also has the multiple colors of the previous vase and the terra cotta appearance. $450+

Leaf and Berry Bud Vase, 7" high, Tharaud porcelain mark 1.1 in green, 1920-1945, and Tharaud decorating mark 3 in blue, 1920-1945. The beauty of this vase is in its simplicity with drooping leaves and berries. The stems are green and the leaves and some of the berries are outlined in gold. $125

"Terra Cotta" Vase, 15.5" high, Tharaud porcelain mark 1.1, 1920-1945, and Tharaud decorating mark 2 in blue, 1920-1945, with *MADE IN FRANCE* in blue, and artist signed, *J. de Brito*. This is a stunning vase of grapevines and grapes with a terra cotta appearance. $600+

Blue Floral Vase, 11" high x 9" in diameter, Tharaud porcelain mark 1.1 in blue, 1920-1945, and Tharaud decorating mark 2 in blue, 1920-1945. This vase is another stunning example of Tharaud's "connoisseur" pieces, although this vase has less of a "terra cotta" appearance than the previous ones. $600+

Above: Undecorated Lamp Base, 13" high, Tharaud porcelain mark 2.1 in green, 1920-1945. This lamp base is undecorated and unglazed. There is a round hole in the bottom that is curved and finished by the factory, which indicates that this piece was intended to be a lamp base rather than a vase. We have seen one pair of finished lamps in this same blank. Note the figures in relief in the porcelain. $125-$150

Above right: Pair of Blue Portrait Vases, 9.5" high, Délinières porcelain mark 2, 1891-1900. These vases are decorated under the glaze, and they are definitely factory decorated. According to Richard Rendall (an experienced collector in Ohio), the portrait on the right, "The Lady with the Muff," is Julie Mole-Raymond, the celebrated 18th century actress of the Comedie-Francaise. The oil on canvas original was painted by Elisabeth Vigee-Lebrun, the court painter to Marie Antoinette. We do not know the identity of the portrait on the left. The quality of the decoration on these vases is superb. Pair, $700+

Right: Footed Portrait Vase, 12" high, Martial Redon porcelain mark 2, 1882-1890, and Dresden decorating mark in blue, and decorated by the Ambosius Nicholaus Lamm decorating studio, c. 1891-1896. This piece is decorated with intricately raised gold and enamel, and the neoclassical figures are in 18th century dress. $1,400+

Filigree Decorated Vase, 3.75" high, Gérard, Dufraisseix & Morel porcelain mark 1, 1881-1890. Although the vase does not bear a decorating mark, the vase is definitely factory decorated; and the decoration is over the enamel, which gives it a dull bisque finish. This vase has the same decoration as the demitasse set featured on page 95 with the Tressemanes & Vogt decorating mark 2, from the early 1880s-1891. $65-$85

Right: Vine Handled Vase, 11.75" high, Délinières porcelain mark 1.1, c. 1870s-1891. This vase is factory decorated, even though there is no decorating mark. The handle, a vine with applied porcelain flowers, is unique and fits the decorating theme of the vase. Vases from this period with applied decorations are scarce. $300-$400

Rooster Handled Vase, 13.75" high, Bawo & Dotter decorating mark 2 in red, c. 1870-c. 1880s. This is a fine example of an early Bawo & Dotter vase, which is hand painted with colors of turquoise, dark blues, and heavy use of gold. Note the rather unrefined handles, which are typical of this period. $400-$500

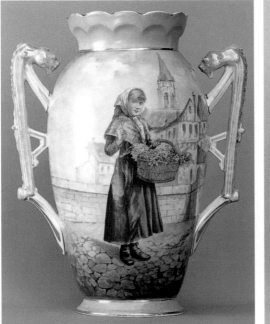

Left: Lion Handled Vase, 13.25" high, Bawo & Dotter decorating mark 2 in red, c. 1870-c. 1880s. This is an early figural vase decorated with both transfers and hand painting. The front, which depicts a girl, is mostly transfers with hand painted highlights, while the back is all hand painted. It has very unusual and rather primitive lion headed handles. $350-$400

Above: Eagle Handled Vase, 7.25" high, Bawo & Dotter decorating mark 2 in red, c. 1870-c. 1880s. This is another example of an early animal handled vase, which is well decorated and completely hand painted. Note the gold leaf butterfly. All flowers, leaves and vines are outlined in gold. $150-$175

Above left: Figural Vase, 7" high, Redon porcelain mark 2, 1882-1890, and artist, *Wagner*. According to Richard Rendall (an experienced collector in Ohio), there were 16 Wagners who painted in the Dresden studios at the turn of the twentieth century. There is no way to link up the name Wagner to any particular person, since there are no available records. Nevertheless, the Wagner name is associated with fine portrait painting on German porcelain. The porcelain on this vase is very translucent, almost "eggshell" in thickness. $500-$600

Left: Figural Vase, 8.75" high, Guérin porcelain mark 4, 1891-1932, and Guérin decorating mark 5 in blue, 1891-1932. This scene was a very popular transfer pattern. This same transfer appears on the charger decorated by a different company, Maas, on page 24. We have also seen this transfer on a washbasin and pitcher. $250-$300

Above & Above right: Exotic Bird Urns, 18.5" high, Le Tallec decorating mark 3 and μ, 1972, with artist, *GM*. The name of this pattern is *Princesse Astrid*. This is a pair of superb and majestic urns with matched scenes of a parrot and cockatoo on one side and unmatched scenes of water birds on the other. Both urns are meticulously hand painted. Pieces of this size are not common and are very expensive. $5,000+

Right: "Mythology" Vase, 10.6" high, Raynaud porcelain mark 10, from 1960 and in use in 1979, and Raynaud decorating mark 9, from 1960 and in use in 1979. This piece is decorated with transfers, and we are uncertain of the identity of the mythological character on the front. $100-$150

19

Hummingbird Vase, 6.5" high, Limoges porcelain mark 21 in green, current, and Alice & Charly decorating mark 2 in black, c. 1999-present. The name of this pattern is *Colibri* (hummingbird), and this vase is entirely hand painted by Nizète German, signed *N. Inacio 2000*, who is one of the most talented decorators now working in Limoges. (See background information on Ms. German on page 148.) $425-$450

Butterfly Vase, 7.5" high, Alice & Charly decorating mark 2 in black, c. 1999-present, and marked *Exclusively S&D Limoges*, and signed, *N. Inacio* (Nizète German) *2000*. The hand painting is exquisite. The name of the pattern is *Le Papillion*. See comments under previous vase. $650-$675

Owl Bud Vase, 6.75" high x 8.5" from head to tail, *Limoges/Peint Main* (hand painted) in script. There is no way to date this piece from the mark, but we feel it is a newer piece. We have included it because this is a complete owl figurine that is also a bud vase with multiple holes in the back. The blank is unusual. $50-$75

Two Dubois Chargers, "Two Lovers in Forest," 15.5" in diameter, Lazeyras, Rosenfeld & Lehman decorating mark 1, 1920s; "Roman Couple," 15.25" in diameter, Klingenberg decorating mark 4, 1891-1894. Although hand painted pieces by Dubois are relatively abundant, these two chargers represent some of the better *Dubois* decorated pieces. (Tardy, see Bibliography, lists several Dubois decorators during this period—Dubois, 1867-1897; Dubois, 1903-1929; and Dubois, 1904-1907. Many of the *Dubois* signed pieces, however, appear to have the same signature, but we are unable to identify which Dubois was the decorator.) The figures are well proportioned, and there is a sense of mood in both of the paintings. Dubois was almost certainly an independent artist, because his paintings appear on pieces with the decorating marks of many different companies. Most of his pieces seem to date from the 1890s-1920s. Each, $1,000-$1,400

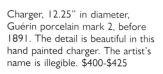**Above & right:** Full Portrait Charger, 12.25" in diameter, Blakeman & Henderson decorating mark 2 in red, c. 1890s, artist signature illegible. This is a well-executed frontal full-length portrait. $450+

Charger, 12.25" in diameter, Guérin porcelain mark 2, before 1891. The detail is beautiful in this hand painted charger. The artist's name is illegible. $400-$425

Jockey on Horse Charger, 13" in diameter, Limoges porcelain mark 5 and signed by A. (Ted Alfred) Broussillon, 1859-1922. This is one of the better hand painted Limoges chargers with an unusual subject matter. $400-$500

Young Girl Portrait Charger, 13.5" in diameter, Gérard, Dufraisseix & Morel porcelain mark 1, 1881-1890. Although this plate was probably not decorated by a professional studio, the portrait is a fine example of arts and crafts painting during the late 1890s. It appears that the androgynous child is a commoner in the French Revolution, as indicated by the clothing and stormy background. We have seen similar portraits on other Limoges pieces. $300+

Colonial Couple Plate, 11.5" in diameter, Borgfeldt decorating mark 1, 1906-1920. This plate is an example of a typical colonial theme, which was common over several decades in Limoges. The artist, Luc, was very prolific and painted many Borgfeldt pieces. The quality of the decoration of a large number of Borgfeldt pieces is mediocre to poor, although there are some exceptions. The quality of the decoration of this piece is average. $275-$300

Tavern Scene Charger, 18" in diameter, Borgfeldt decorating 1 in blue, early 1900s-c.1920 and signed, *Dubois*. Chargers of this size are rare. This charger is also unusual because it has a hand painted scene, which includes numerous people. The interaction of the people in the tavern is well done. $1,500-$1,800

Colonial Couple Charger, 12.5" in diameter, Maas decorating mark 1, 1894-c.1930. This is the same transfer as that on the Guérin vase on page 18. Pieces decorated by Maas are difficult to find. $300+

Framed Portrait Charger, 13" in diameter, Lazarus Straus & Sons decorating mark 1 in blue, c. 1890s to mid-1920s, and sticker with S. *MASS/Limoges/FRANCE*, 1894-c. 1930. This charger is unusual in a number of respects. From the sticker, we know that this piece was decorated for the U.S. importer, Lazarus Straus & Sons, by the Limoges decorating firm, S. Maas. Usually, we only see the decorating mark of Lazarus Straus & Sons and not the mark of a particular Limoges decorator. The blank has an unusual border of leaves and flowers and the background in the porcelain is in the shape of a coat of arms. In terms of decorating style, it is not common to find a "framed" portrait in the center of the charger and the use of a fading solid color. See the S. Maas decorated cup and saucer on page 100 to see a similar use of a solid color for decoration. $400-$600

Four-Girl Charger, 13" in diameter, Flambeau decorating mark 3 in green, 1890s-c. WWI. This charger is hand painted and signed, *Dubois*. $300-$400

Above: Soustre Portrait Tray, 17.75" in diameter, T. Haviland decorating mark p, 1903-1924, and two T. Haviland paper labels that are partially illegible (see labels, above right). The title of this piece is "Solitude," a theme that was widely copied on porcelain by the Wagner family at KPM Berlin and other artists at Dresden and Thuringia. This piece was decorated by Antoine Soustre, who was one of the finest porcelain painters in Limoges. Although he painted many pieces for the T. Haviland Company, he was probably an independent artist because he also painted pieces on blanks from other companies. Also, there are no records from the T. Haviland Company that indicate Soustre was employed by them. In this case, the tray, or blank, was most likely made by St. Cloud, with the trim decorated by T. Haviland. (Some of the above information about A. Soustre comes from a conversation with Wallace J. Tomasini, Ph.D., a Haviland expert at The University of Iowa.) A. Soustre is able to reflect a mood or feeling in the portrait, which is further enhanced by the background; and this painting is a fine example of his work. $2,000+

Nude Charger, 12.5" in diameter, Flambeau decorating mark 2 in red, 1890s-c. WWI, and signed, *Dubois*. Completely nude figures, other than cherubs, are not common and are highly sought after by collectors. Some pieces with nudes command very high prices. $1,200+

Left: Bird Charger, 13.5" in diameter, Limoges porcelain mark 1 and Lazeyras, Rosenfeld & Lehman decorating mark 2 in green, 1920s. Bird chargers were a common theme in the late 1890s-1920s, and this is a typical example. This piece is hand painted by Muville and has the characteristic heavy gilding around the edge. $350-$400

Right: Bird and Floral Charger, 12.6" in diameter, R. Haviland porcelain mark 1, 1924, and Madesclaire decorating mark 1 in green, used in 1929. It is unusual to find a charger totally decorated with transfers and accented with a heavily gilded border. Pieces with the Madesclaire decorating mark are not common. $150-$175

Left: Bird Charger, 13" in diameter, C. et J. mark 1, c. late 1800s-1914. C. et J. is an unidentified Limoges company. The painting was done by Ted Alfred Broussillon, 1859-1922, one of the better Limoges painters of game birds and flowers. The artistic appeal of this piece is the artist's use of white to set the mood for the painting. The birds are white breasted, feeding on the white snow covered ground, with white snow flurries in the sky, and tree branches partially covered with white snow. The birds themselves appear alive, busily searching for food. Also notice the use of heavy gilt around the border. This piece is one of the best examples of the popular theme of game birds in Limoges in the late 1890s and early 1900s. As with many of the Limoges chargers painted c. 1900-1920s, it appears that the outlines were made with engraved transfers before the pieces were painted. We have seen many Limoges chargers with the same paintings, including this one by Broussillon. $450+

Hunting Dog Charger, 10.25" in diameter, Paroutaud decorating mark 2, 1902-1916, and signed, *E. Golie* (partially illegible). $150-$175

Serving Plate, 12.75" in diameter, Délinières porcelain mark 2, 1879-1900, and Délinières decorating mark 4, 1879-1900. This plate is interesting because of its size, the details and shape of the blank, and the use of purple flowers. $75-$100

Fox Charger, 13" in diameter, Coiffe porcelain mark 3, after 1891, and Lazarus Straus & Sons decorating mark 1 in green, c. 1890s-c. mid-1920s, and signed, *Dubois*. $350-$400

Hunting Dog with Duck Charger, 18" in diameter, Limoges porcelain mark 3 and Flambeau decorating mark 5 in green, c. late 1890s-c. WWI, and signed, *J. Marsay*. This hunting scene is a common subject on Limoges chargers during this period, but hunting scenes are not currently popular, especially those with dead game animals. This is an unusually large size. $750-$850

Cow Charger, 10" in diameter, Flambeau porcelain mark 1, c. late 1890s-c. WWI, and Flambeau decorating mark 2, c. late 1890s-c. WWI, and signed, *PAL.* $150-$175

Two Seafood Plaques, 13.5" x 10.5", Coiffe porcelain mark 2, after 1891. Although these plaques are not factory decorated, the hand painting is excellent. There is no artist's signature. Set, $400-$500

Castle and Fruit Charger, 12.5" in diameter, Royal decorating mark 1, and signed, *J. Soustre.* $175-$200

Seascape Charger, 13" in diameter, Comte d'Artois mark 1. (This is not the mark of the original Comte d'Artois from the late 1700s.) The artist's signature looks like *L. Mure,* although the spelling is not certain. This is an interesting blank, with a detailed gilded border. We have noticed that chargers with this blank command relatively high prices. $325-$400

Limoges Plates

May Day Plates and Cup/Saucer, plates, 10.4" in diameter; cup, 2.5" high x 4" in diameter and saucer, 7.25" in diameter, Vignaud porcelain mark 5, 1938-1970, and decorating mark, *Guy Thirion/Décor Main/Paris/France*, in blue with the word, *Mai*, (French for the month of May, maypole, and May Day) on the bottom and top of the saucer. Guy Thirion, a decorating in studio in Paris, hand decorated these dinnerware pieces. We believe that these pieces represent May Day celebrations, although we are unsure of the significance of the ships. Note the masquerade costumes of the three characters. The theme of these pieces is unusual and the quality of the decoration is exquisite. We do not have any information about the Guy Thirion decorating studio. $250-$300

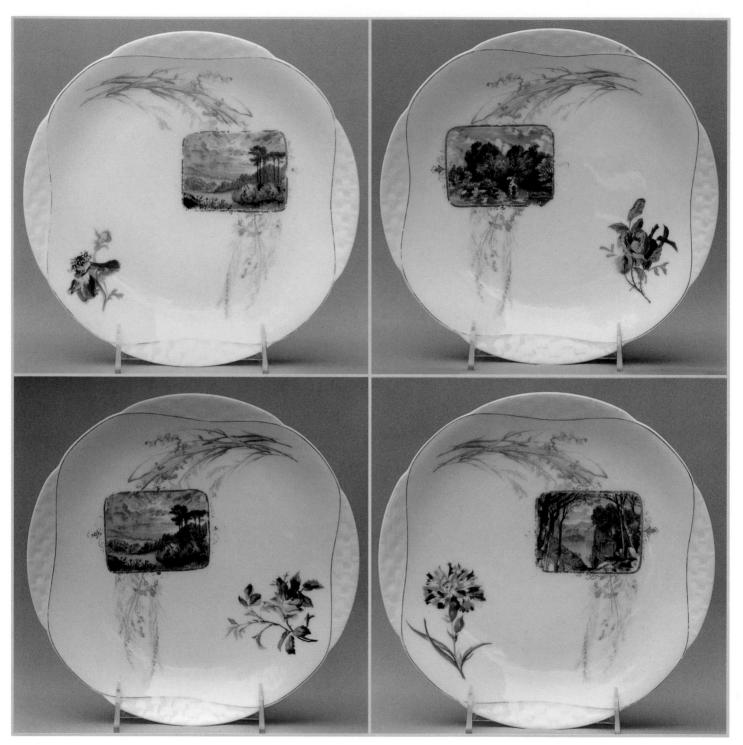

Blue Scenic Plates and Demitasse Cups/Saucers, plates, 8.5" in diameter; cups, 2.25" high x 2.1" in diameter and saucers, 4.75" in diameter, Haviland & Co. porcelain mark c. 1876-1879, on the demitasse set and mark F, 1876-1889, on the plates and Haviland & Co. decorating mark g, 1879-1889, on all pieces. Entirely hand painted, the decoration is unusual with a different individual scene painted as part of a larger design of flowers and what appears to be wheat spikes. Note the hand painted detail in the close-ups of two of the scenes on the demitasse cups. Each plate, $50-$60, and each demitasse cup/saucer, $40-$60 (continued on next page)

Dessert Plates, 8.5" in diameter, T. Haviland decorating mark j in red, probably 1892. These eight plates are all hand painted. Set, $800-$1,000
(continued on next page)

Floral Plate, Blakeman & Henderson decorating mark 2 in red, c. 1890s. This hand painted plate is a good example of the border decoration enhancing the pattern of the blank. The flowers are very well painted. $250+

Plate, 8.75" in diameter, T. Haviland porcelain mark M impressed, 1894-1957, and T. Haviland decorating mark q, 1903-1924. This plate is lavishly decorated with gold and blue leaves around the outside, which are then contrasted with a simple and typical Haviland floral pattern. There is something incongruent between the vibrant colors of the hand painted gold and blue decoration and the simple pale floral pattern. $55-$65

Floral and Gold Plate, 9" in diameter, Haviland & Co. porcelain mark F, 1876-1889, and Haviland & Co. decorating mark g in brown, 1879-1889. This is a very well decorated plate combining floral transfers and hand painted highlights. $75-$125

Victorian Couple Plate, 9" in diameter, Vultury Frères porcelain mark 1, 1897-1904, and Blakeman & Henderson decorating mark 2 in red, c. 1890s. The pattern of the shell accented blank is quite beautiful. $125-$175

Parisian Service Plate, 9" in diameter, Haviland & Co. porcelain mark D, 1876-1886, and Haviland & Co. decorating mark g, 1879-1889. This plate is one of 12 plates in a series called the Parisian Service, which was designed by Félix Bracquemond. Bracquemond worked for Sèvres before joining the Paris workshop of C. É. Haviland from 1872-1880. He was inspired by Japanese art and heavily influenced ceramic design in Limoges during this period. The original Parisian Service was manufactured in 1876, and the plates were signed by Bracquemond. Each of the plates represents a "moment" during a time of the year, and each is depicted with birds in the countryside. This service was reissued two years later in 1878, and this plate, which is one of the 12 of the Parisian Service, is called *Soleil Couchant* (Setting Sun). Although this plate is not signed and was most likely one of those reissued in 1878, it is still very rare and highly collectible. $1,000-$1,500

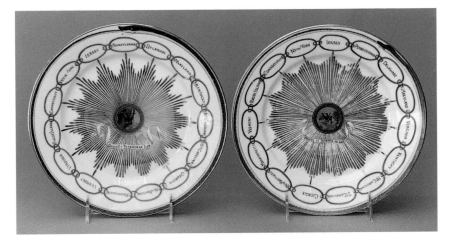

U.S. Centenary Plates

First color plate, 8.5" in diameter, T. Haviland porcelain mark Q, 1946-1962, and T. Haviland decorating mark s in gold, 1958-1967, and *Martha Washington* in script in gold. An insert that accompanied this plate, reads as follows: "This plate is a replica of the one that Haviland & Co. was commissioned to manufacture, in 1876, to celebrate the Centenary of the Signing of the Declaration of Independence of the United States of America. The original set of china, known as the 'MARTHA WASHINGTON' or 'STATES' china, was a gift to Lady Washington, in 1796, from Andreas Everardus Van Braam Houckgust, A Dutchman and Representative of the Dutch East India Company. The original service consisted of about 45 pieces and was made in China, on special order, for presentation to the First Lady. The decoration is composed of a circular chain containing the names of the fifteen states of the Union, at that period. Vermont and Kentucky were added to the original thirteen States in 1791 and 1792, respectively. The snake, holding its tail in its mouth, is a Chinese symbol of continuity and symbolizes the perpetuity of the Union. The interlaced letters of the monogram, M.W., are set against a sunburst of gold and the Latin motto, on a red scroll, 'Decus Et Tutamen Ab Illo', stands for, 'Honor and Protection come from Him'. Edition is limited to 2500..." $50

Second black and white plate is a photograph of the original plate taken from the d'Albis book (see Bibliography).

Third color plate, 8.75" in diameter, T. Haviland porcelain mark M impressed, 1894-1957, and T. Haviland porcelain mark L in brown, 1893. Note the close-up of the snake. $200

Fourth color plate, 8.6" in diameter, S&S porcelain mark 1, and *R.H. Macy & Co./New York* inside oval in black. This plate is similar to the others, but the snake is in a slightly different position and the ordering of the states is different. This plate is definitely factory decorated. It appears that several pieces in this pattern were produced around 1893, which may indicate that they were made to commemorate the 100th anniversary of Martha Washington's term as First Lady (1789-1793). We have also seen a similar plate, 7.5" in diameter, marked *Dulin and Martin Co./Washington, D.C.* in red. See following teapot. $150-$225

U.S. Centenary Teapot, 5.75" high x 7.75" from spout to handle, Guérin porcelain mark 0.5 impressed, from c. 1870s, and Guérin porcelain mark 4, 1891-1932. This teapot, which has the same theme as the previous plates, was probably decorated during the same period, based upon the dating of the two porcelain marks. Although there is no decorating mark, this piece was definitely professionally decorated. $200-$300

Courtesy of The White House

Above and left: President Hayes Service Plate, 9" in diameter, Haviland & Co. porcelain mark D, 1876-1886, and Haviland & Co. decorating mark a, prior to 1876. Other markings include, *Design Patented August 10th 1880 No. 11932*, in blue; the signature, *Theo. R. Davis*, in black; and the presidential eagle (see photo). Based upon the markings on the back of this plate, this piece from the President Hayes Service was actually used in the Arthur and Cleveland administrations. This plate of a Passenger or Wild Pigeon—now extinct—is pictured (see photo) in the book on White House china by Margaret Brown Klapthor (see Bibliography). $700+

Egyptian Plate, 8.25" square, Gérard, Dufraisseix & Morel porcelain mark 1, 1881-1890. This plate is one of the more unusual designs of the "Egyptian Plates," which were probably part of a fish set. It is unclear whether all of the decoration on this plate was done by the factory. The umbrella with the eagle is a recurring symbol in Egyptian art. $150-$175

Egyptian Plate, 8.25" square, Gérard, Dufraisseix & Morel porcelain mark 1, 1881-1890, and Gérard, Dufraisseix & Morel decorating mark 2 in blue, 1881-1890. This plate also represents an unusual design of the "Egyptian Plates" and further suggests that these plates were part of a fish set. Note the detail on the four corners. $150-$175

Ridged Oyster Plate, 8.6" in diameter, T. Haviland porcelain mark L, 1893-1894, and decorating mark, *Manufactured by Théodore Haviland for Burley & Company/Chicago* in red. (Burley & Co. was a wholesaler, retailer, and decorator of china and was based in Chicago. They were in operation from 1837-1931.) The blank for this oyster plate is unique. It is designed with raised seaweed highlighted with gold, and the oysters are placed between the leaves. These oyster plates are quite rare. $350+

Oyster Cup, 1" high x 2.9" x 3.25", Délinières porcelain mark 2, 1891-1900, and Délinières decorating mark 4 in red. Individual oyster cups are scarce, and the ones that we have seen have all been manufactured by either Délinières or Haviland & Co. They are shaped like an oyster, with ridges on the under side which correspond to the ridges of an oyster shell. See the section on white blanks for an undecorated photograph of this same oyster cup. $75-$85

Oyster Plate, 7.5" in diameter, Gérard, Dufraisseix & Morel porcelain mark 1, 1881-1890, and Gérard, Dufraisseix & Morel decorating mark 2 in red, 1881-1890. The gold highlighting on this plate emphasizes the pattern in the blank. $150-$200

Asparagus Plate, 6" in diameter, Gérard, Dufraisseix porcelain mark 1, 1890-1900, and Gérard, Dufraisseix decorating mark 2 in red, 1890-1900. The single well on this plate is used for the sauce. Asparagus plates are not easy to find. $175+

Dinner Plate, 9.9" in diameter, Demartial porcelain mark 2.1, 1891-1893, and Demartial decorating mark 3, 1891-1893, and *Tiffany & Co/New York* in green. This is an unusual decorating style, with the scenic transfers and the thick hand painted gold accents. Set of six plates, $300-$375

Plates, 9.7" in diameter, Guérin porcelain mark 4, 1891-1932, and Guérin decorating mark 7 in red, 1891-1932, and artist signed *H. Desprez*. The first plate is titled on the back, *Ussé*, and the second plate is titled, *Chaumont*. The hand painting of the castle scenes on these cobalt bordered plates is exceptionally well done. Each, $400-$450

Reticulated Floral Plate, 9.1" in diameter, Tressemanes & Vogt porcelain mark 8, 1892-1907, and Tressemanes & Vogt decorating mark 7 in red, 1892-1907, with the words, *MONT JOVIS*, over the bell. Not only are the reticulated edges of the blank unusual, but the plates are entirely hand painted by the factory. These plates would have commanded a high price when they were initially sold. Set of six, $300-$400

Above & below: "Scalloped" Plates, 9.1" in diameter, Haviland & Co. porcelain mark G, 1887, and Haviland & Co. decorating mark g in brown, 1879-1889. Decorated on the "Cannelé" blank, these plates could be used for any kind of meat or poultry. (According to Wallace J. Tomasini, Ph.D., the Cannelé blank "was an ingenious transformation of the Japanese chrysanthemum plate." See Bibliography.) We have seen four of these plates, each with a different animal; it is possible that a complete set was made up of 12 different kinds of animals and birds. What is unusual is that these kinds of sets were usually designed exclusively for serving either game birds, fish or meats; the designs were not usually mixed. Also, these plates are entirely hand painted. Set of two, $150-$200

Toucan Plate, 8.9" in diameter, T. Haviland porcelain mark M impressed, 1894-1947, and T. Haviland decorating mark p, 1903-1925. Although the decoration is all transfer, the plate is really stunning. This is an unusual T. Haviland subject. $85-$100

Thanksgiving Plates, 10" in diameter, Ahrenfeldt decorating mark 7, 1896 and after, and CAR decorating mark 1. The transfer decoration on these plates is unusually ornate and striking. It is not common to find dinner-sized plates with a turkey/Thanksgiving theme; most plates with this theme are the smaller dessert/luncheon size. Both plates, $150-$185

Hand Painted Bird Plates, 9.5" in diameter, Klingenberg porcelain mark 9, 1895-1916, and Klingenberg decorating mark 7 in red, 1895-1916. Entirely hand painted, these plates were decorated as art objects and not to be used as dinnerware. Each plate is signed, *Roche*, followed by the number *96*. These plates are very well painted, and the artist used very bright colors, which is unusual for bird plates before 1900. Set of four, $300+

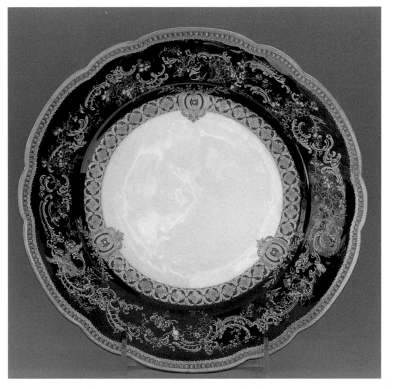

Bird Plate, 9" in diameter, Haviland & Co. porcelain mark H, 1888-1896, and Haviland & Co. decorating mark c in red, 1876-1878/1889-1931, with *FOR BURLEY & COMPANY/Chicago* in red. This plate is entirely hand painted on a very well designed blank. The red and gold painting highlights the pattern in the porcelain around the edge of the plate. There is no signature. $200

Above & below: Cobalt Plate, 9.25" in diameter, Haviland & Co. porcelain mark I, 1894-1931, and Haviland & Co. decorating mark c in red, 1876-1878/1889-1931. This is probably the best decorated cobalt plate that we have seen. Notice the intricate detail around the rim with small hand painted birds as part of the design. $175-$200

Napkin Fold Plate, 8.5" square, Haviland & Co. porcelain mark F, 1876-1889, and Haviland & Co. decorating mark g, 1879-1889. The details in the porcelain blank are very intricate. According to Wallace J. Tomasini (see Bibliography), the Napkin Fold design "is another Western variation on a possibly Japanese type…" $75-$85

Ice Cream/Dessert Plate, 6.75" square, Gérard, Dufraisseix & Morel porcelain mark 1, 1881-1890, and Gérard, Dufraisseix & Morel decorating mark 2, 1881-1890. All of the gold decoration is hand painted, and the design is quite typical of this period. Set of 12, $250-$400

Cake Plates: Changes in Decorating Styles from c. 1860-mid-1920s

These cake plates are illustrative of the changes in the decoration of dinnerware during the period from the 1860s to the late 1920s. The earlier pieces are for the most part, except for C. F. Haviland Plates 1 and 2, muted transfer floral patterns, which are similar to the well-known early Haviland & Co. multiflorals, such as Old Blackberry, Old Pansy, etc. There is a charm in the simplicity of these early patterns. The decoration of the Haviland & Co. Meadow Visitors Cake Plate 5 expands beyond the simple floral patterns of the other early plates.

The C. F. Haviland Plates 1 and 2, on the other hand, appear to be among the earliest of these plates because of the almost monochrome color of the decoration. Cake Plate 15 represents the transition from the muted floral patterns to those that are more colorful. Beginning with Cake Plate 17, which was probably decorated at the very beginning of the 20th century, the colors become more vibrant and the patterns more pronounced. We start seeing many lavishly hand painted and hand accented cake plates, from about 1900 to the 1920s, beginning with Cake Plate 18. Cake Plate 20, which probably dates from the late 1920s, was decorated with transfers and represents dinnerware which was mass marketed, unlike Cake Plates 18 and 19, which were predominately hand painted.

Cake Plate 1, 10.75" handle to handle, C. F. Haviland porcelain mark 3, c. 1865-1881, and C. F. Haviland decorating mark 1 in blue, 1881 and before. $60-$75

Cake Plate 2, 10.75" handle to handle, C. F. Haviland porcelain mark 3, c. 1865-1881, and C. F. Haviland decorating mark 1 in blue, 1881 and before. $60-$75

Left: Cake Plate 3, 10.25" handle to handle, Bawo & Dotter decorating mark 2, c. 1870-c. 1880s. $40-$60

Right: Cake Plate 4, 10.25" handle to handle, Bawo & Dotter decorating mark 3, c. 1870-c. 1880s. $40-$60

Meadow Visitors Cake Plate 5, 10" handle to handle, Haviland & Co. porcelain mark D, 1876-1886, and Haviland & Co. decorating mark g, 1879-1889. $60-$85

Cake Plate 8, 10" handle to handle, Haviland & Co. porcelain mark F, 1876-1889. Although there is no decorating mark, this plate is definitely factory decorated. $40-$60

Cake Plate 6, 9.6" handle to handle, Haviland & Co. porcelain mark F, 1876-1889, and Haviland & Co. decorating mark g, 1879-1889. The handles on this plate are not cut out like the other cake plates in this section. $40-$60

Cake Plate 9, 10" handle to handle, Délinières porcelain mark 1, c. 1870s-1891. Although there is no decorating mark, this plate is definitely factory decorated. $40-$60

Cake Plate 7, 10.5" handle to handle, Lanternier decorating mark 1.1 in red, before 1890. This plate is entirely hand painted with bright colors. The handle shape is unusual. $40-$60

Cake Plate 10, 10.25" handle to handle, Tressemanes & Vogt decorating mark 1.1, 1880s-1891. $40-$60

Cake Plate 13, 10" from handle to handle, Guérin porcelain mark 2, before 1891, and Guérin decorating mark 5 in red, 1891-1932, with *Made For R.J. ALLEN SON & CO/PHILA-DELPHIA, Pa.* $40-$60

Cake Plate 11, 10.25" handle to handle, Tressemanes & Vogt decorating mark 2.1 in blue, with *86* in center, 1880s-1891. The decoration includes hand painted white accents. $40-$60

Cake Plate 14, 10.9" handle to handle, S&S porcelain mark 1 and Lazarus Straus & Sons decorating mark 1, c. 1890s-mid-1920s. $40-$60

Left: Cake Plate 12, 10.75" handle to handle, Pouyat porcelain mark 7, 1891-1932, and Pouyat decorating mark 6 in red, 1890s. $40-$60

Right: Cake Plate 15, 10.25" from handle to handle, Bawo & Dotter porcelain mark 11, 1896-1920, and Bawo & Dotter decorating mark 8 in red, 1896-1920. Note the cut out handles. $40-$60

Cake Plate 16, 10.5" handle to handle, Délinières mark 2, 1891-1900, and Bernardaud decorating mark 4 in red, 1900-1978, and *HIGGINS & SEITTER/NEW YORK* in red. $40-$60

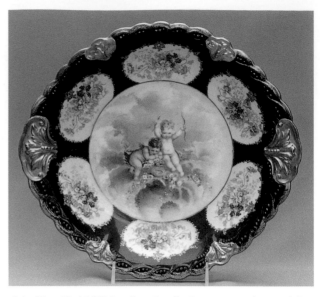

Cake Plate 18, 11.25" handle to handle, Limoges porcelain mark 3 and Lazarus Straus & Sons decorating mark in red, c. 1890s-mid-1920s. This cake plate is decorated with a combination of transfers and hand painting. $250+

Cake Plate 17, 10.75" handle to handle, Laviolette porcelain mark 1, 1896-1905, and Burley & Co. decorating mark 1, 1885-1931. (Although Burley & Co. was a wholesaler, retailer and decorator of china based in Chicago, they also had pieces labeled and decorated for them in Limoges, with a Limoges mark. They were in business from 1837-1931.) $50-$65

Cake Plate 19, 11.75" handle to handle, P.M. Mavaleix porcelain mark 1, c. 1908-1914, and Borgfeldt decorating mark 1, 1906-1920, and artist signed, *A. Broussillon* (Ted Alfred Broussillon, 1859-1922). This is an entirely hand painted cake plate by one of the better Limoges painters of game birds and flowers. $250+

Cake Plate 20, 10.6" handle to handle, Haviland & Co. porcelain mark I, 1894-1931, and Haviland & Co. decorating mark i, 1926-1931. $50-$60

Portrait Plate, 10.25" in diameter, Haviland & Co. porcelain mark D, 1876-1886. Although there is no mark, the plate was definitely professionally decorated. The portrait is hand painted, but there is no artist's signature. This plate is exquisitely decorated. $700-$850

Portrait Plate, 9" in diameter, Guérin porcelain mark 4, 1891-1932, and Guérin underglaze decorating mark 4.5, 1891-1932, with *Feu de Four*. Feu de four refers to a technique where the paint is applied directly on the raw unbaked porcelain and fired at higher than normal temperatures. Bleu de four is the same technique but refers to cobalt. "Four" refers to the "main whiteware kiln and not to the muffle kiln normally used for the firing of décor." Feu de four pieces were made from the late 1870s to the late 1880s. Relatively few of them were produced because they were not commercially successful. They were originally sold at much higher prices. $200-$275

Portrait Plate, 8.4" in diameter, Pouyat porcelain mark 7, 1891-1932, and overglaze in red script, *8482/Peinture grand feu de four/J. Pouyat Limoges*. This is a rare individually handwritten decorating mark from the factory, and attests to the fact that feu de four pieces were not made in large numbers. This piece is signed by the artist, *Goodillou*. $200-$300

Blue Accented Plate, 8.5" in diameter, Haviland & Co. porcelain mark H, 1888-1896, and two Haviland & Co. decorating marks c, 1876-1878/1889-1931, one in black, with *"Feu de Four,"* and the other in red, with *For/Cha*ˢ *MAYER &Cᵒ/Indianapolis*, inside a donut shaped mark. The decoration of this plate is very odd. The feu de four decoration in blue appears as random "splotches" which are overlaid by a hand painted ornate gold pattern. The blue decoration appears almost as though it were an accident. $125-$150

Floral Plate, 8.5" in diameter, Haviland & Co. porcelain mark H, 1888-1896, and two Haviland & Co. decorating marks c, 1876-1878/1889-1931, one in black, with *"Feu de Four,"* and the other in red, with *FOR BURLEY & COMPANY/CHICAGO*. The decoration of this plate is more traditional. The feu de four firing results in subtle but striking pink flowers. $125-$150

Christmas Nativity Plate, 8.6" in diameter, Ancienne Manufacture Royale (Société Porcelainière) porcelain mark 13, used in 1972, and Ancienne Manufacture Royale (Société Porcelainière) decorating mark 13.5, used in 1972, with *Noël/The Nativity, "Les santsons de Noël"/(Little Christmas Saints)*. This piece was designed by Roch Popelier, and it is marked No. 1 in a series. $25-$35

Series of One Christmas Plate, 8.25" in diameter, T. Haviland porcelain mark U in red, beginning in 1957, and in overglaze black script, *Made exclusively for Sale in Great Britain only*. This 1971 Nöel Christmas plate was the first in what was to be a series of 12 plates for the British market, but it was not a commercial success, so the subsequent 11 plates were never produced. Although there is no artist's name on the back, the design is similar to that of the T. Haviland Christmas plate series, 1970-1981, sold in the U.S., which was designed by Remy Hétreau. Note that the plate for the British market came out in 1957 versus 1970 for the first plate in the U.S. series. This plate is very scarce. $200+

Series of Two Christmas Plates, 9" in diameter, T. Haviland decorating mark t, beginning in 1967. In what was intended to be a series of six Christmas plates, only the plates in the first two years, 1986 and 1987, were produced. The first plate is marked, *1986, No. 1, Deck the Hall with Boughs of Holly, of 6*, and the second plate is marked, *1987, No. 2, Hark the Herald Angels Sing, of 6*. It is also written on the back of the plates that they were a limited edition and were designed by Elisa Stone. Each, $75-$100

Christmas Plate, 9.75" in diameter, Lanternier porcelain mark 5, 1891-1914, and Lanternier decorating mark 6 in brown, 1891-1914. Pieces decorated with holly and ivy are very collectible and difficult to find. $75-$100

Series of Five Bicentennial Plates, 9.75" in diameter, T. Haviland porcelain mark Q, 1946-1962, and T. Haviland decorating mark t, beginning in 1967. These richly decorated series of five plates, 1973-1976, were designed by Remy Hétreau to celebrate the U.S. bicentennial. Hétreau also designed the T. Haviland Christmas plate series from 1970-1981. The bicentennial series is as follows: Burning of the Gaspee, 1772/1972; Boston Tea Party, 1773/1973; First Continental Congress, 1774/1974; The Ride of Paul Revere, 1775/1975; and The Declaration of Independence, 1776/1976. Series of five, $125-$150 (continued on next page)

Canape Plate, 6" in diameter, Deshoulières decorating mark 1, current, with artist, Marie-France Lecherbonnier. There are a series of six canapé plates, representing the five senses. Each plate has a different figure. Set of six, $100

Above & below: Pitcher or Creamer, 6.75" high, Haviland & Co. porcelain mark A impressed, 1853—. For one of the earliest Haviland & Co. pieces, this pitcher is elegantly decorated. Note the feathery gold effect on the spout. $175-$200

Pitcher, 11" high, Alluaud mark 1 impressed, 1881 and before. This piece is important because the Alluaud mark is extremely rare, and the piece is in excellent condition. François Alluaud became the director in 1788 of what was the original porcelain factory in Limoges, soon after the factory was purchased by King Louis XVI in 1784 who made it a subsidiary of Sèvres. In 1798/1799 F. Alluaud started his own factory but died the following year, when his son, also named François, took over. Charles Field Haviland took over the Alluaud factory in Casseaux in 1876. This pitcher may have been part of a bathroom set that would have included a basin, chamber pot, and other pieces. $400+

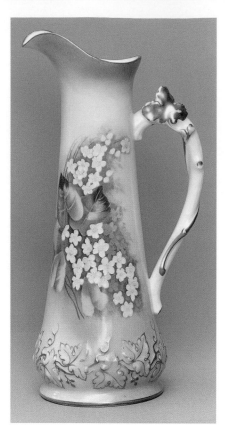

Pitcher/Wine Decanter, 12" high, Tressemanes & Vogt porcelain mark 10, 1892-1907, and Tressemanes & Vogt decorating mark 12 in purple, 1907-1919. This piece is well decorated with a combination of transfers and hand painted highlights. Note the gold applied leaf on the handle. $200-$225

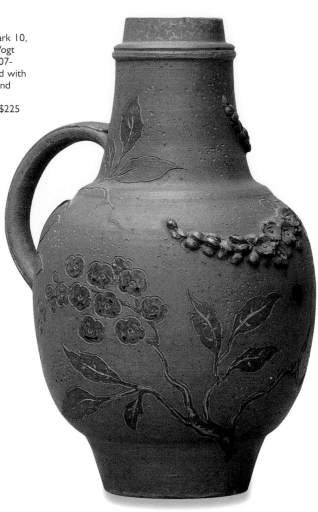

Wine Jug, 11.25" high, Haviland & Co. porcelain mark X impressed (Chaplet mark), 1883-1885. Chaplet was a ceramist with Haviland & Co. from 1876 to 1885. This stoneware piece also has two artists' initials, B and G. This piece has an almost primitive appearance, with raised flowers and flowers and leaves which have been painted. Chaplet pieces are highly collectible. $1,500-$2,000

Left: Large Pottery Ewer, 13" high, Haviland & Co. porcelain mark V impressed, 1875-1882, signed, *E.* (Edouard) *Lindeneher,* on bottom in black and impressed, *eL,* on side. Lindeneher was a ceramic sculptor for Haviland from 1875-1893. This ewer is one of the nicest examples of Haviland's earthenware *(faïence)* line, because it is relatively large and is decorated with applied leaves and flowers. The decoration of much of the earthenware was inspired from Japanese designs and the impressionist movement (Wallace J. Tomasini, Ph.D., see Bibliography). Haviland's production of faïence during this period had a limited life span because it was not a commercial success. $1,500-$2,000

Pitcher, 13.25" high, Délinières porcelain mark 2, 1891-1900, and Dresden decorating mark in blue. This hand painted pitcher was decorated by the Richard Klemm studio, c. 1888-1916, and signed, *Kaufman*. Both the scene and the gold work are exquisite. $1,400

Wine Jug, 7.5" high x 6.5" in diameter, Haviland & Co. porcelain mark D, 1876-1886, and Haviland & Co. decorating mark g in blue, 1879-1889. Also marked *2873* in gold and signed, *Boilvin*, under portrait. Boilvin began working for Haviland around 1872. The decoration is transfers with hand painted enamel highlights. Wine jugs are not common. $600-$800

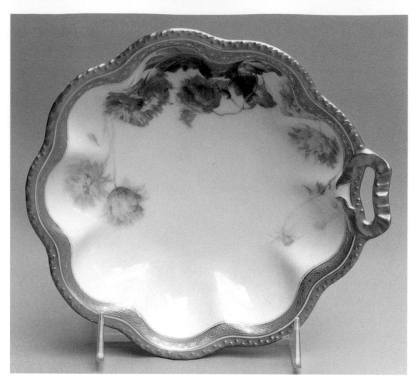

Open Bowl, 8.4" in diameter, Haviland & Co. porcelain mark I, 1894-1931, and Haviland & Co. decorating mark c in green, 1876-1878/1889-1931, with *"Feu de Four"* in green. For comments about feu de four, see earlier description of Guérin portrait plate on page 51. $150-$200

Bowl, 6.25" high and 12.75" handle to handle, Laporte porcelain mark I in green, c. 1883 and *OVINGTON BROS* in brown. Laporte pieces are rarely seen in the U.S., which indicates that not many were exported. This is an exquisite piece, with an intricate blank. It is decorated on the outside with hand painted yellow and gold highlights and gold thistle transfers. The inside is hand painted cherry blossoms. Yellow was not a commonly used color during this period. $500-$700

Above & below: Open Vegetable Dishes, first vegetable, 3.1" high x 7.25" x 8.75," and second vegetable, 2.5" high x 8.6" x 10.25," Haviland & Co. porcelain mark F, 1876-1889, and Haviland & Co. decorating mark c in red, 1876-1878/1889-1931. The blanks are very well designed. Each, $125-$150

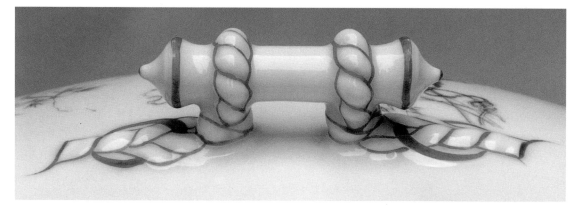

Two Covered Vegetable Bowls, 5.75" high x 11.5" long, Haviland & Co. porcelain mark D, 1876-1886, and F, 1876-1889, and Haviland & Co. decorating mark g in black, 1879-1889, and *2023-1* in red. These are exceptionally well decorated covered vegetable serving bowls in the cable shape, with flowers and even a turtle on one of them. Note the orange detail on the handles. Examples of this cable shape are more frequently seen decorated with gold bands. Each, $200-$250.

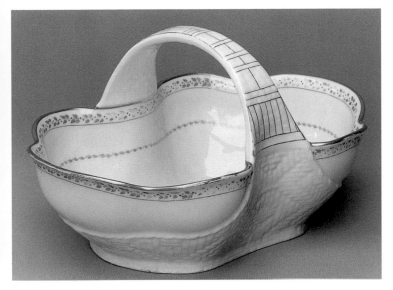

Platter, 13" x 10.25", Bernardaud decorating mark 7 in gold, current, with *Reine Elisabeth/Service exécuté pour la réception en France de S.M. La Reine Elisabeth/Avril 1957* in gold. This service was in honor of Her Majesty Elizabeth II's visit to France in 1957. We have seen a complete dinner service in this pattern. $150-$200.

Fruit Basket, 7.25" high x 11" x 7.5", Haviland & Co. porcelain mark D, 1876-1886, and Haviland & Co. decorating mark g in green, 1879-1889. Although the decoration on this basket is quite simple, the blank is very well designed and difficult to find. $225-$275

Green Dragon Punch Bowl, 8.75" high with stand x 9.1" in diameter, Tressemanes & Vogt porcelain mark 10, 1892-1907, and Vogt decorating mark 12 in purple, 1907-1919. Factory decorated punch bowls are not common. Most Limoges punch bowls in the U.S. are decorated by amateur painters in floral, berry, or fruit patterns. This punch bowl and stand are decorated with a combination of transfers and hand painting. $900+

Platter, 13.4" x 20," Haviland & Co. porcelain mark F, 1876-1889, and Haviland & Co. decorating mark g in brown, 1879-1889. This is a magnificent platter, because of its size and the pattern of the blank. $200-$250

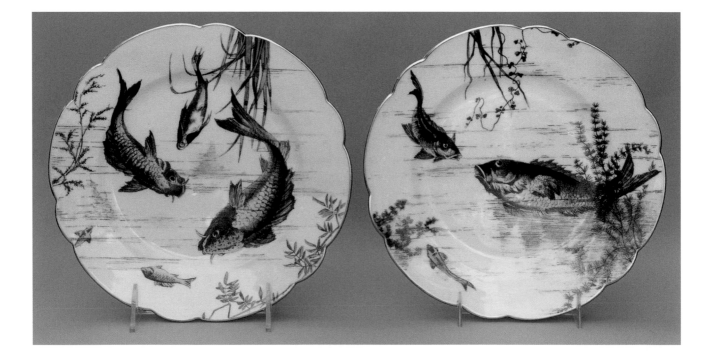

Fish Set, platter, 16" x 10" and plates, 8.25" in diameter, Tressemanes & Vogt porcelain mark 3, c. 1891, on platter and Délinières porcelain mark 1.1, c. 1870s-1891, on the plates and Tressemanes & Vogt decorating mark 2.1 in blue, c. 1891, on all pieces. This set was probably decorated around 1891, since one of the pieces has the Délinières porcelain mark and the rest have the early Tressemanes & Vogt porcelain mark. Tressemanes & Vogt purchased their first porcelain manufacturing facilities in 1891; before this time, the company was only a decorating studio. This Tressemanes & Vogt decorating mark is not common. This set represents an early example of a fish set, which is extremely well decorated, yet does not show the use of bright colors that appeared on fish sets in later years. Set with platter and 12 plates, $1,000+

Platter and Plates, platter, 16.25" x 9.5" and plates, 7.5" in diameter, Pouyat porcelain mark 3, c. 1876-1890, and Pouyat decorating mark 4 in red, c. 1876-1890. The decorating style of this set is interesting. Although the entire scene covers each piece, part of the scene is framed by using darker colors and filling in the sky. The effect is a picture within a picture. These pieces are entirely hand painted. Set with platter and 9 plates, $1,500-$2,000

Platter, Covered Bouillon Cups/Saucers and Covered Sauce Tureen with Attached Underplate, platter, 20" x 12"; bouillon cups, 3.5" high x 3.25" in diameter and saucers, 5.1" square; and covered tureen, 4" high x 8.25" x 5.1", Gérard, Dufraisseix & Morel porcelain mark, 1881-1900, and Gérard, Dufraisseix & Morel decorating mark 2 in blue, 1881-1900. This is a magnificent set, with the handles and finials exquisitely hand painted with a gold design. Pieces shown, $700-$900

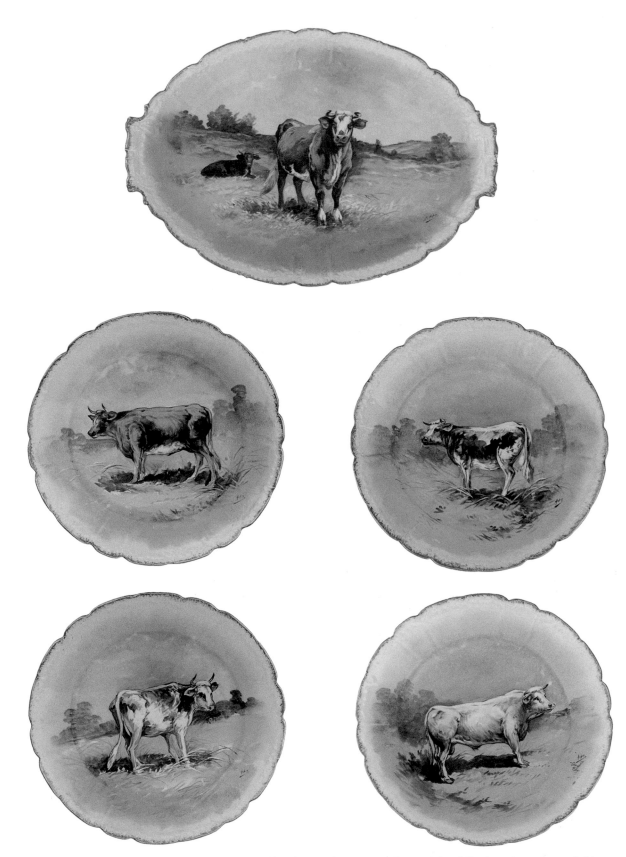

Cow Platter and Plates, platter, 21" x 16" and plates, 10" in diameter, Limoges porcelain mark 3 and Flambeau decorating mark 5 in green, c. late 1890s–c. WWI, and artist signed, *Aubin*. These pieces are entirely hand painted, and the subject matter is rare. Most sets of this kind are of game animals and not domestic animals. This set has four variations of the plates as shown. Set with platter and 12 plates, $1,800-$2,200

Platter/Tray, 2.25" high x 9.4" x 13.75", Gérard, Dufraisseix & Morel porcelain mark 1, 1881-1890. A sticker on the back reads, *J Seth Hopkins &Co/CHINA/ GLASS/ HOUSEKEEPING/CUTLERY/FANCY GOODS/ BALTIMORE.* This piece is entirely hand painted, and it appears that it was decorated at the factory. The painting is exceptionally well done, and the tray has four matching plates that were not photographed. Tray, $250-$350

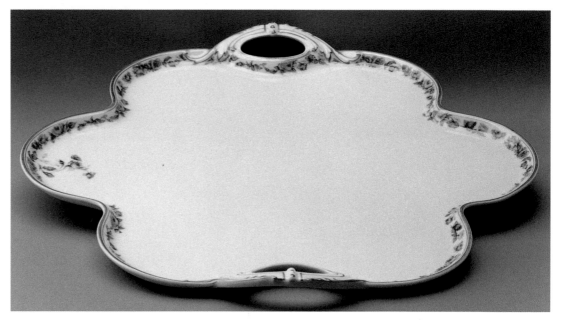

Serving Tray, 18" x 17.75", Haviland & Co. porcelain mark 1, 1894-1931, and Haviland & Co. decorating mark h in red, 1892-1931. This is a very large and well decorated serving tray with the border trimmed in floral transfers. $300-$375

Bread Tray, 3.5" high x 6" x 13.75," Haviland & Co. porcelain mark 1, 1894-1931, and Haviland & Co. decorating mark c in red, 1876-1878/1889-1931, with *FOR J.M. & W. Westwater. ESTAB-LISHED 1840 Columbus Ohio* in red. This bread tray has a noteworthy "boat" shape. $175-$200

Bread Tray, 7.25" x 13.75", Haviland & Co. porcelain mark I, 1894-1931, and Haviland & Co. decorating mark c in red, 1876-1878/1889-1931. This is one of the more unusual and collectible Haviland patterns. $200-$250

Bread Tray, 7.25" x 13.75", Haviland & Co. porcelain mark I, 1894-1931, and Haviland & Co. decorating mark c in red, 1876-1878/1889-1931. This blank is similar to the previous blank, except it has a reticulated edge. $175-$200

Open Dish, 9.75" handle to handle, Haviland & Co. porcelain mark I, 1894-1931, and Haviland & Co. decorating mark c in red, 1876-1878/1889-1931. This is the same as the red/pink "Drop Rose" pattern but only in gray. Pieces in this color are highly collectible. $200-$250.

69

Open Vegetable Dish, 2.25" high x 10.25" x 7.4", Porcelaine Limousine porcelain mark 1, 1906-1938, with *M. REDON/Limoges/Made Expressly for/DULIN & MARTIN/WASHINGTON/D.C.* in red. This is a very simple but classic serving dish with dull gold trim. $50-$70

Open Vegetable Bowl, 10" in diameter, Martin & Duché porcelain mark 1, after 1891, and Martin & Duché decorating mark 4 in blue, used in 1929. $50-$75

Floral Dish or Soup Bowl, 9.5" in diameter, Ahrenfeldt porcelain mark 11, c. 1896 and after, and Ahrenfeldt decorating mark 11.5, c. 1896 and after, with *C. REIZENSTEIN/PITTSBURGH-ALLEGHENY* in brown. The name of the artist looks like *YIREITH*. This piece came from an expensive service, because it is hand painted, signed by the artist and the base rim underneath is painted gold. $175-$225

Vegetable Bowl, 3" high x 10.5" in diameter, Le Tallec decorating mark 3 and τ, 1975, and artist, *mc*. The name of the pattern is *Cartels Attributs Musique Bouquet Central*. This is a stunning hand painted piece with lavish raised gold accents and flowers and four different musical instruments. $500-$600

Three-Footed Dish, 3.1" high x 7.4" in diameter, Le Tallec decorating mark 3 and *WW*, 1965, and artist *AM*. The name of the pattern is *Carousel Chinois*. This piece is superbly decorated with six different Chinese figural scenes. $500-$700

Covered Dish, 7" high x 8.5" handle to handle, Le Tallec decorating mark 3 and *TT*, 1963, with artist, *SF*. The name of the pattern is *Grignan Vert*. The etched and painted gold accents along with the swan handles make this a stunning dish. $800-$1,000

Platter and Plates, platter, 8.5" x 15" and plates, 7.25" in diameter, Haviland & Co. porcelain mark F, 1876-1889, and Haviland & Co. decorating mark g in blue, 1879-1889. Although all the plates have a slightly different floral pattern, they all match the pattern on the platter. This set is a beautiful example of one of Haviland's multifloral patterns, with hand painted enameled highlights. Platter and 10 plates, $500-$600

Part of Very Early Haviland & Co. Set, platter, 14" x 10"; casserole, 10.25" handle to handle x 7" high; and cups, 2.5" high x 2.4" in diameter and saucers, 4.75" in diameter, Haviland & Company mark A impressed, from 1853—, on casserole only. According to Nora Travis (see Bibliography), only the larger pieces of dinnerware sets were marked during this period, and Haviland did not routinely mark all of their pieces until 1871. We know that the other pieces here are Haviland because they came from the same set and have the same raised porcelain ivy pattern with gold accents and burgundy bands. The finial of the casserole is a molded artichoke highlighted with gold. (According to d'Albis, see Bibliography, these pieces were designed by Labesse for Haviland & Co. and were shown in the Haviland catalogue of c. 1865. This set was called the *Artichaut* [Artichoke] service.) Pieces from this period are very rare, and cups and saucers from this period are even scarcer. Set as shown, $600+

Part of Very Early C. F. Haviland Set, gravy with detached underplate, 4.5" high x 9.75" x 6.4"; bowl, 4.1" high x 10.25" in diameter; cup, 3.1" high x 3.5" in diameter and saucer, 6.25" in diameter; large open dish, 2.3" high x 11.1" x 8" at widest point; and relish, 1.5" high x 9" x 4.9" at widest point, C. F. Haviland porcelain mark 1 impressed on gravy, open dish and relish, and no marks on other pieces. The unmarked pieces are from this same set, before the company began marking all of its pieces. Pieces from this period are scarce. Set as shown, $450+

Above & right: Dinner Set, dinner plates, 10.25" in diameter; salad/dessert plates, 7.75" in diameter; and demitasse cups, 2.25" high x 2.25" in diameter and saucers, 4.6" in diameter, Le Tallec decorating mark 3 and α, 1967, and ß, 1967, with the artists, *CC, AD,* and *FG.* The pattern, *Marin* (yellow/gold), on these pieces is decorated with lead based paste for the relief. Because of the lead in the relief, the pattern, which is still being produced today, is hand engraved with an agate stone. Place setting for 12, $8,000+

Covered Vegetable, 8" high x 8.5" in diameter, Le Tallec decorating mark 3 and *DF,* 2000, and *CS.* There is no pattern name, since this piece was specially made to complement rather than match the previous pieces in the *Marin* pattern. $250+

Octagonal Covered Vegetable, 7" high x 9.75" in diameter, Le Tallec decorating mark 3 and *DF*, 2000, and *CS*. Like the previous vegetable dish, this piece was almost made to complement the *Marin* pattern. $325+

Place Setting, cup, 1.9" high x 3.6" in diameter and saucer, 5.5" in diameter; dessert plate, 8.25" in diameter; and dinner plate, 10" in diameter, Limoges porcelain mark 1, and *SAKS-FIFTH AVENUE/MADE IN FRANCE* in black. The shape and pattern of the blanks are stunningly set off with minimal gold trim. Set as shown, $225-$250

Lobster Dish, 11.5" x 9.5", Haviland & Co. porcelain mark F, 1876-1889. Although this dish is not factory decorated, the hand painted decoration is far superior to most pieces decorated by the Haviland & Co. factory. The painting follows and enhances the pattern in the porcelain. $200-$250

Toothpick Holder, 2.1" high x 2.4" in diameter at the base, Haviland & Co. porcelain mark H, 1888-1896. These toothpick holders are scarce and highly collectible. This one is in the Ranson blank. $75-$125

Double Egg Cup, 3.6" high x 2.5" in diameter, Haviland & Co. decorating mark h in red, 1893-1931, and also marked, *Made for J.A. Baillargeon & Co./Seattle Wash.* This is a double egg cup, the smaller end for a single egg and the larger end for two eggs. $50-$75

Salt and Pepper, 4" long x 1.5" high, F&F mark 1. These European style salt and pepper in the shape of snails are well decorated with floral transfers and gold highlights. $30-$40.

Mustard Pot, 3" high x 4.25" in diameter, Gérard, Dufraisseix & Abbot porcelain mark 6, 1900-1953, and Gérard, Dufraisseix & Abbot decorating mark 9 in red, from 1941-1976. $50-$70

Child Food Warmer, 2" high x 7.25" square, Raynaud porcelain mark 4, 1952-1960, and Raynaud decorating mark 7, from 1950, and *Walt Disney Productions* in orange. Child food warmers are not easy to find. $100-$125

Tea Caddy, 3.5" high x 3.5" x 2.25", Pairpoint decorating mark 1, c. 1880s. As is characteristic of most Pairpoint decorated Limoges pieces, the decoration on this tea caddy follows and enhances the pattern of the blank. The Pairpoint company, located in New Bedford, Massachusetts, is well known for its glass and silver artwork. It is probable that their decoration of Limoges porcelain was limited to the period of the 1880s. $225-$250

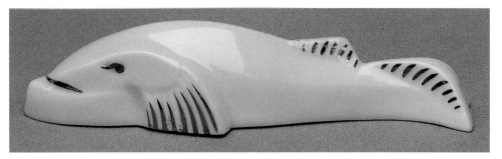

Knife Rest, 5" long, Thabard mark 1, 1932-c. 1950. Relatively few Thabard pieces are available because the factory was in business for only a relatively short time. This piece is a uniquely designed knife rest. $25-$30

Multifloral Compote, 5.4" high x 8.5" square, Haviland & Co. porcelain mark F, 1876-1889, and Haviland & Co. decorating mark g in blue, 1879-1889. This piece is a good example of one of Haviland's multifloral patterns, and compotes in good condition are one of the harder multifloral pieces to find. $100-$125

Sauce Boat with Detached Underplate, 3.75" high and plate, 8.75" x 5" at widest point, Haviland & Co. porcelain mark C, 1876-1879, and Haviland & Co. decorating mark g in black, 1879-1889. This sauce boat with the underplate in the Meadow Visitors pattern is highly collectible. $175-$225

Covered Sauce Tureen with Attached Underplate, 4.6" high x 9.5" x 5.75", Haviland & Co. decorating mark g in black, 1879-1889. This piece, like the previous one, is highly collectible. $175-$225

Cheese Dish, lid, 5" in diameter and plate, 6.25" square, Gérard, Dufraisseix & Morel porcelain mark 1, 1881-1890, and Gérard, Dufraisseix & Morel decorating mark 2 in blue, 1881-1890. The cover, finial, and plate have an Egyptian motif. There is a hole in the top under the finial. These cheese dishes are not common. $150-$200

Cheese Dish, 6.9" handle to handle, Gérard, Dufraisseix porcelain mark 1, 1890-1900, and Gérard, Dufraisseix decorating mark 2 in red, 1890-1900. Like the previous piece, this is an unusual cheese dish. Note the hole in the top under the finial. $150-$200

Pancake Dish, 9.1" in diameter, Gérard, Dufraisseix & Morel porcelain mark 1, 1881-1890, and Gérard, Dufraisseix & Morel decorating mark 2 in black, 1881-1890. Pancake dishes are very much in demand by collectors, and this is a very fine example of one. People frequently confuse cheese, butter and pancake dishes. $175-$225

Bonbon Dish, 6.75" in diameter x 2.5" high, Bawo & Dotter porcelain mark 11, 1896-1920, and Bawo & Dotter decorating mark 8 in red, 1896-1920. Although this is a common blank, there are not many of these blanks that are factory decorated. This particular blank was popular with amateur painters in the U.S. during this same time period, 1896-1920. $50-$60

Candlesticks, 8.75" high, Bernardaud porcelain mark 3, 1900-1978, and Pickard decorating mark, 1919-1922. These candlesticks are simple but elegant, and they are decorated in etched gold, which is one of Pickard's signature designs. $200+

Three-Section Serving Dish, 11.6" x 11.4", Limoges Castel porcelain mark 2, used in 1950-1979+. This dish is decorated with gold peacock transfers, and all three sections are different sizes. $35-$45

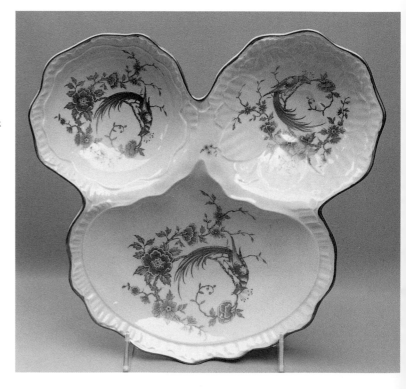

Limoges Coffee and Tea Service

Coffee and Dessert Set, coffee pot, 8.5" high; tray, 7.6" x 10.5"; sugar, 1.9" high x 3.5" in diameter; creamer, 3.75" high at handle; dessert plates, 7.5" in diameter; coffee cups, 2" high x 3.75" in diameter and saucers, 5.75" in diameter; and demitasse cups, 1.9" high x 2.25" in diameter and saucers, 4.4" in diameter, Le Tallec decorating mark 3 and Z, 1953, and AA, 1954, with the artists, *mc* and *clc*. The demitasse set and the dessert plates are also marked, *Monsieur Louis Hand*, the individual for whom the set was decorated. Le Tallec has no records to identify Monsieur Hand. The pattern is called *Dentelle on gold* and is no longer made because the paste for the white relief contains lead. As with all Le Tallec pieces, everything is hand painted. Note the details of the relief on the coffee and demitasse cups, and the relief on the inside rim of the coffee cup. This coffee set is elegant. Complete coffee and dessert set for six, $5,500+

Coffee Set, cup, 2.4" high x 2.5" in diameter and saucer, 4.75" in diameter; creamer, 4.75" high; and sugar, 5.75" high, Tharaud porcelain mark 1.1, 1920-1945, and Tharaud decorating mark 3 in blue, 1920-1945. Tharaud dinnerware pieces decorated using special firing techniques (see comments under Tharaud vases) are rare. Set, including seven cups and saucers, $600-$750

Dessert/Luncheon Set, cup, 2.1" high x 3" in diameter and saucer, 5.6" in diameter; cake plate, 10.5" handle to handle; and dessert/luncheon plate, 7.4" in diameter, C. F. Haviland porcelain mark 3, 1865-1881. Although this set has no decorating mark, these pieces were definitely factory decorated. The gold pattern on this set was a very common decorating style during this period, and it was used by both Haviland & Co. and C. F. Haviland. Set as shown, $100-$125

Dinnerware Set, coffee pot, 9.75" high; pitcher, 8.75" high; two smaller pitchers, 4" and 5" high; cup, 2.4" high x 2" square and saucer, 4" square; plate, 9.25" square; and covered vegetable, 11" handle to handle, Haviland & Co. porcelain mark F, 1876-1889, and Haviland & Co. decorating mark g in blue, 1879-1889. This is a magnificent dinnerware set. The simple gold highlights emphasize the well-designed and unusual blanks. For the pieces shown, $1,000+

Dessert/Luncheon Set, cup, 2.1" high x 3.5" in diameter and saucer, 5.6" in diameter; cake plate, 9.5" in diameter; and dessert/luncheon plate, 7.4" in diameter, Haviland & Co. porcelain mark C, 1876-1897, and Haviland & Co. decorating mark g in black, 1879-1889. This pattern is more commonly seen with gold accents. Pieces with the maroon accents are scarcer. Note that the accents match the color of the flower transfers. $150-$175

Individual Coffee Set, coffee pot, 4.75" high; creamer, 3.5" high; and sugar, 3.5" high, Haviland & Co. porcelain mark F, 1876-1889, and Haviland & Co. decorating mark g in green, 1879-1889. A three-piece individual coffee set in a matching Meadow Visitors pattern on the butterfly handled blank is scarce. Note that the butterfly transfers complement the butterfly handles. Set of three, $250+

Chocolate Pot, 9" high, Haviland & Co. porcelain mark D, 1876-1886, and Haviland & Co. decorating mark g in green, 1879-1889. The gold accents on the anchor handle, spout, and finial make this an attractive example of the Meadow Visitors pattern. Note the interesting shape of the blank. $200-$300

Four Legged Creamer, 4.75" to top of handle, Haviland & Co. decorating mark d in blue, 1879-1883, and *Davis Collamore & Co/ Broadway and 21st Street/New York* in blue. This coffee set is called "Torse." This is a very unusual and rare blank. $150-$200

Teapot, 9.4" handle to spout, Haviland & Co. porcelain mark G, 1887, and Haviland & Co. decorating mark g in green, 1879-1889. This teapot has an unusual shape. $150-$175

Coffee Set, coffee pot, 9.75" high; sugar, 6.5" high; creamer, 5.6" high; and cup, 2.75" high x 3" in diameter and saucer, 5.5" in diameter, Lanternier decorating mark 1.1 in blue, before 1890. Although each piece has many different floral patterns, the subjects that pull the set together are the scenes of the castle, wooden fence, and the swan, which are repeated individually but not all together, on the different pieces. This is an interesting design technique used by several companies in the late 1800s. All the pieces are decorated with transfers. Set, including eight cups/saucers, $600+

Tea Set, teapot, 6.75" high x 9.5" spout to handle; sugar, 5" high x 7" handle to handle; and creamer, 4.5" high x 6" spout to handle, Tressemanes & Vogt porcelain mark 8, 1892-1907, and Tressemanes & Vogt decorating mark 15 in purple, 1907-1919, with *Made for R.J. Allen Son & Cº/Philadelphia* in purple. This tea set has the typical early muted floral transfers, with interestingly angled handles. $225-$250

Coffee Set, coffee pot, 8.5" high; creamer, 5.5" high; and sugar, 6.5" high. Pouyat decorating mark 4 in red, 1876-1890. This set, which also includes two dessert plates, two bowls, and two cups and saucers (not pictured), is a very good example of the muted multifloral patterns used during the last quarter of the 19th century. The shapes of the porcelain handles and finials are particularly interesting in this set. Complete set, $400-$450

Tea Set, T. Haviland decorating mark j in red, probably beginning in 1892, the first T. Haviland decorating mark. The gold highlighting and transfers complement the pattern in the blanks. $300-$375

Coffee Set, coffee pot, 9" high, Bawo & Dotter porcelain mark 11, 1896-1920, with *Made in France for Higgins & Seiter/New York* in red. The combination of the footed creamer and sugar, the exquisite gold accents, and the placement of the floral pattern against both the red and white backgrounds make this a very attractive set. $300+

Coffee Set, coffee pot, 6.75" high; creamer, 2.6" high; and sugar, 8.4" high, T. Haviland porcelain mark P, 1926-1945, and T. Haviland decorating mark r, 1925-1957, and marked, *Décor de Solange Patry-Bié*, and the pattern, *MAYFLOWER*. S. Patry-Bié was a decorator for T. Haviland from 1935-1968. Although the decoration of these pieces is typical "40s," the nontraditional porcelain molds illustrate a willingness to experiment with different shapes. Set, $250-$350

Art Deco Coffee Set, coffee pot, 7.75" high x 6.75"; creamer, 5.25" high x 6.75"; sugar, 5.5" high x 9"; and cup, 2.1" high x 3.5" in diameter and saucer, 5.75" in diameter, Descottes, Reboisson & Baranger mark 1, 1922-1927, and *JACOMART & CIE/244 et 248/ RUE Léon Gambette/ LILLE* in red. This is an exquisite example, in terms of both the shape of the porcelain and the decoration, of the art deco style. The porcelain manufacturer was only in business for six years. We are not familiar with the decorating studio. Set as shown, $275-$400

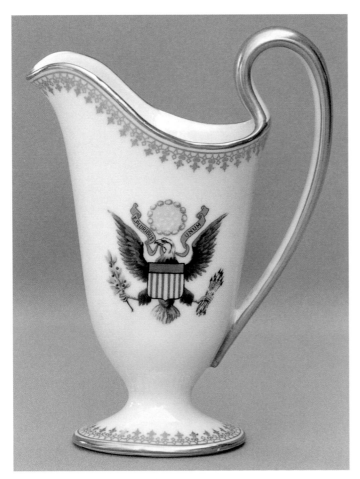

Creamer, 5.5" high, Tressemanes & Vogt porcelain mark 10, 1892-1907, but decorated by Raynaud after he took over the Vogt company in 1919, and marked over the glaze in blue, *The National Remembrance Shop, Washington, D.C.* Pieces with this Great Seal of the United States had to be special ordered from the Raynaud factory, and this seal is very similar to the one used on dinnerware made by Knowles, Taylor & Knowles of East Liverpool, Ohio, for President McKinley, 1897-1901. $50-$55

Limoges Cups and Saucers

Demitasse Cup/Saucer, cup, 2.4" high x 2.25" in diameter and saucer, 5" in diameter, Bawo & Dotter decorating mark 2 in red, c. 1870-c. 1880s. This set is a great example of pieces, during this period, that are entirely hand painted and heavily decorated with gold. Many Gutherz pieces were similarly decorated during this time period. $75-$125

Demitasse Cup/Saucer, cup, 1.5" high x 2.25" in diameter and saucer, 4" in diameter, Klingenberg decorating mark 4 in red, 1891-1894. This set is also heavily decorated with gold, and the porcelain is paper thin. $40-$70

Five Demitasse Cups/Saucers, cups, 2.25" high x 2.1" in diameter and saucers, 4.25" in diameter, Haviland & Co. porcelain marks D, 1876-1886; F, 1876-1889; and G, 1887, and overglaze mark, *Geo. C. Shreve & Co./San Francisco*. These pieces are representative examples of Haviland & Co.'s demitasse cups and saucers in the last quarter of the 19th century. Because these cups and saucers are over 100 years old, there are relatively few complete sets of eight or more. When used today, matching cups and saucers of different patterns are often mixed. Note that the saucers are shaped like small bowls and they do not have an indentation for the cup. This is characteristic of many demitasse saucers during this period. Each, $40-$60

Demitasse Cup/Saucer, cup, 2.25" high x 2.25" in diameter and saucer, 4.5" in diameter, Tressemanes & Vogt porcelain mark 8, 1892-1907, and Tressemanes & Vogt decorating mark 5 in purple, 1892-1907, and *Pitkin & Brooks/Chicago* in purple. The blanks for both the cup and saucer are very well designed, with the cup resting on ridges on the bottom. $40-$60

Demitasse Cup/Saucer, cup, 2.1" high x 2.1" in diameter and saucer, 4.6" in diameter, Tressemanes & Vogt decorating mark 2 in purple, 1880s-1891. This same pattern was produced in at least two additional colors—pink and gold. The small gold bands on the cup—on the top of the rim, inside near the rim, and at the base—indicate that this was an expensive pattern. $40-$60

Three Footed Demitasse Cups/Saucers, cups, 2.5" high x 2.4" in diameter and saucers, 4.75" in diameter, Haviland & Co. porcelain mark E ,—1877, and Haviland & Co. decorating mark g in green, 1879-1889. Along with the gold painted feet, the decoration of solid colors on the insides of these cups is quite striking. Each, $60-$85

Cup/Saucer and Plate, cup, 1.6" high x 3.6" square and saucer, 5" square; and plate, 7" square. Haviland & Co. porcelain mark D, 1876-1886, and Haviland & Co. decorating mark g in brown, 1879-1889. The napkin fold design of this porcelain pattern carries over to a uniquely shaped cup and saucer. These cups and saucers are scarce. Set, $175-$225

Cups/Saucers, cups, 2" high x 3.5" in diameter and saucers, 5.75" in diameter, T. Haviland decorating mark p, 1903-1925. This set is decorated in solid bright colors. Each, $50-$65

Cup/Saucer, cup, 1.6" high x 3.6" square and saucer, 5" square, Haviland & Co. porcelain mark F, 1876-1889, and Haviland & Co. decorating mark g in blue. This is the same blank as the set in the previous photo. $150-$200

Demitasse Cup/Saucer, cup, 2.1" high x 2.25" in diameter and saucer, 4" in diameter, Haviland & Co. mark H, 1888-1896, and overglaze mark, Haviland & Cº/For/MEYBERG BROS/LOS ANGELES, CAL. This demitasse cup has a very unusual shape. $40-$60

Demitasse Set with Case, cups, 2.25" high and saucers, 4.5" in diameter, Délinières porcelain mark 1.1, c. 1870s-1891, and Tressemanes & Vogt decorating mark 2, 1880s-1891. This complete set of 12 demitasse cups and saucers are stored in a cloth lined protective leather case. These cased sets were often given as wedding gifts. Since Tressemanes & Vogt decorated these pieces on Délinières blanks, it seems likely that these pieces were decorated prior to 1891 when Tressemanes & Vogt purchased two small porcelain factories. The decoration on this set is the same as the filigree vase on page 16, which is decorated on the outside of the enamel giving it a dull bisque finish. Additionally, the name on the underside of the lid of the case under the lining is *Haviland & Co.* It seems likely that other Limoges companies, as well as U.S. importers and retailers, purchased these cases separately from Haviland & Co. for use with china from any manufacturer, since most demitasse cups and saucers were of similar size during this period. A complete set of cups and saucers in the original case is quite rare. $800+

Cup/Saucer, cup, 2.1" high x 3.4" in diameter and saucer, 5.5" in diameter, Délinières porcelain mark 2, 1891-1900, and Délinières decorating mark 3 in red, 1891-1900. The transfer decoration on this set carries not only the early multifloral pattern, but also introduces an animal motif. $40-$50

Two Cups/Saucers, both cups, 2.25" high x 3.5" in diameter and both saucers, 5.75" in diameter. The first cup has Gérard, Dufraisseix & Morel porcelain mark 1, 1881-1890, and Gérard, Dufraisseix & Morel decorating mark 2 in black, 1881-1890, and the second cup has Haviland & Co. porcelain mark C, 1876-1879, and Haviland & Co. decorating mark g, 1879-1889. Although both of these cups and saucers are from the same period, note the much higher quality of the decoration of the Haviland & Co. set, which is decorated in one of the better variations of the Meadow Visitors patterns. Cup with brown flowers, $35-$40 and cup with bird and butterfly, $65-$75

Breakfast Cup/Saucer, cup, 2.9" high x 3.9" in diameter and saucer, 6.5" in diameter. Haviland & Co. porcelain mark E, 1877, and Haviland & Co. decorating mark g in blue, 1879-1889. This large cup and saucer is a breakfast cup, and it is decorated with blue trim. $40-$45

Demitasse Cup/Saucer, cup, 3.9" high x 2" square and saucer, 4.75" square. Tressemanes & Vogt porcelain mark 3, c. 1891, and Tressemanes & Vogt decorating mark 5, 1892-1907. What is unusual about this set is the use of the bright yellow and blue colors. The set is entirely hand painted with a raised gold pattern. $40-$60

Demitasse Cup/Saucer, cup, 2.1" high x 2.1" in diameter and saucer, 4.6" in diameter. Délinières porcelain mark 1.1, c. 1870s-1891, and Tressemanes & Vogt decorating mark 5 in red, 1892-1907, with *OVINGTON, BRO'S* in arch over decorating mark. This set was probably decorated before Tressemanes & Vogt purchased their two small manufacturing factories in 1891. As with most pieces decorated for Ovington Brothers, this set is very well done. It is unusual because of the painted pale yellow background. The dull gold leaves are entirely hand painted. $40-$60

Demitasse Cup/Saucer, cup, 2.25" high x 2" in diameter and saucer, 4.5" in diameter. Gérard, Dufraisseix & Morel porcelain mark 1, 1881-1890. Although there is no decorating mark, this set is definitely factory decorated. The forked handle with hand painted accents makes this piece unusual. $30-$50

Demitasse Cup/Saucer, Guérin porcelain mark 2, before 1891. This is a beautifully decorated cobalt and floral vignette cup and saucer. Although not marked, this set is professionally decorated. $175-$200

These five cups and saucers have the Gutherz decorating mark 1 in red, after 1875-1883+. Oscar Gutherz had decorating studios first in Limoges and then later in Austria. Most Gutherz pieces with the Limoges decorating mark do not have a manufacturer's porcelain mark. We have seen, however, one Gutherz dinnerware set with Pouyat porcelain mark 3, c. 1876-1890. Many Gutherz pieces are very well decorated on simple blanks, and these cups and saucers represent some of the best hand painted dinnerware decoration of the late 1800s. The Gutherz studio in Limoges was granted patents on porcelain designs, one as early as 1883, by the United States Patent and Trademark Office (see Henderson in Bibliography). Breakfast cups, $50-$75 each, and tea cups, $40-$50 each

Breakfast Cup, cup, 2.5" high x 4" in diameter and saucer, 6" in diameter.

Breakfast Cup, cup, 2.75" high x 3.75" in diameter and saucer, 6.75" in diameter.

Tea Cup, cup, 2" high x 3.25" in diameter and saucer, 4.9" in diameter.

Breakfast Cup, cup, 2.5" high x 4.2" in diameter and saucer, 6.75" in diameter.

Tea Cup, cup, 2" high x 3.25" in diameter and saucer, 4.9" in diameter.

Portrait Cup/Saucer, cup, 2.5" high x 2.9" in diameter and saucer, 5.5" in diameter, Redon porcelain mark 5, 1891-1896, and Ahrenfeldt decorating mark 2, c. 1891-c. 1896. This set was probably decorated before 1894 when Ahrenfeldt started manufacturing porcelain. This set represents a mixed decorating technique—the portrait is a transfer and the rest of the decoration is hand painted. The name under the portrait is Melle La Valliere, who became a mistress of Louis XIV in 1661 and later in life entered a convent. The decoration on this cup and saucer is exquisite, and the portrait theme is rare. $125-$160

Three Footed Cup/Saucer, cup, 4" high x 2.6" in diameter and saucer, 8.1" in diameter, Le Tallec mark 3, and *ii*, 1958, with artist, *AG*. The name of the pattern could not be identified by Le Tallec. The scenes on the cup and saucer are intricately painted, and this set is done in the Empire style, which was popular from 1804-1820s. $300-$400

Demitasse Cup/Saucer, cup, 1.9" high x 2.4" in diameter and saucer, 4.4" in diameter, Bawo & Dotter decorating mark 4, 1896-1900, and *98* in gold script. This is one of the most intricately hand painted cups and saucers we have seen. There are four unique scenes each on the cup and the saucer. Also note the heavy use of gold. These kinds of pieces are very rare and a serving set is one of a kind. $275-$350

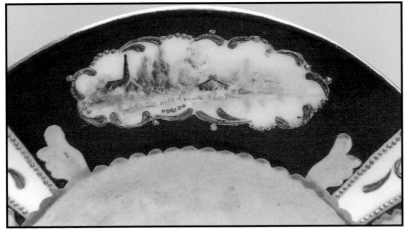

Demitasse Cup/Saucer, cup, 2.1" high x 2.1" in diameter and saucer, 4.5" in diameter, Laviolette porcelain mark 1, 1896-1905, and Bawo & Dotter decorating mark 4 in red, c. 1891-1896. Like the previous demitasse set, the cup and saucer are entirely hand painted, with intricate detailing of the Victorian couple and heavy use of gold to frame the portrait. $175-$200

Demitasse Cup/Saucer, cup, 3" high x 2.25" in diameter and saucer, 4.75" in diameter, Coiffe porcelain mark 2, after 1891, and Klingenberg decorating mark 4 in red, 1891-1894. The all hand painted decoration of the cup and saucer is subtle but striking, and the decoration matches and enhances the pattern in the porcelain. The decoration of this set is superb. $75-$125

Right: Demitasse or Chocolate Cup, 4.4" high, Lazarus Straus & Sons decorating mark 1, c. 1890s-c. mid-1920s. This set is included because the subject, red devils, and the shape of the cup are unusual. Set of three, $75-$100

Cup/Saucer, cup, 2.5" high x 3.5" in diameter and saucer, 5.9" in diameter, Maas porcelain mark 1 impressed, 1894-c. 1930, and Maas decorating mark 2, 1894-c. 1930. This is the first piece that we have seen with *SM* impressed in the porcelain, which would indicated that S. Maas manufactured as well as decorated porcelain. The salmon color shading around the base of the cup and the center of the saucer is an unusual decorating technique. See the M. Maas decorated charger on page 24 and the next cup and saucer for other examples of this decorating technique. $30-$40

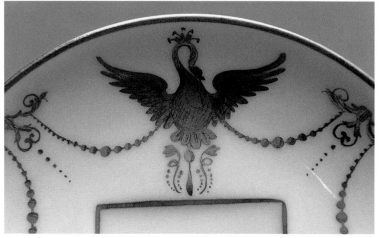

Above two photos: Pedestal Demitasse Set, cups, 2.75" high x 2.75" in diameter and saucer, 4.5" in diameter, Le Tallec decorating mark 3 and *MM*, 1960, with artist, *ML*. The name of the pattern is *Ronde de Cygnes*. The shape of the demitasse cup and the design of the hand painted gold decoration are unusual. Both the base and the handle are painted in solid gold. Set of eight, $1,500+

Demitasse Cup/Saucer, cup, 2.25" high and saucer, 4.5" in diameter, Redon porcelain mark 5, 1891-1896, and Redon decorating mark 3 in red, 1882-1896. The use of shading is similar to the previous Maas decorated cup and saucer, but this set is entirely hand painted. $60-$80

Demitasse Cup/Saucer, cup, 2.25" high x 2.25" in diameter and saucer, 5.1" in diameter. Le Tallec decorating mark 3 and *SS*, 1963, with *Tiffany & C⁰ Private Stock*, and artist, *SHF*. The name of the pattern is *Écailles Roses*. The use of pink and the pattern of the design are atypical. $150

Below: Figures and Dragons Chinoiserie Demitasse Cup/ Saucer, cup, 2.4" high x 2.25" in diameter and saucer, 4.6" in diameter. Le Tallec decorating mark 3 and *PP*, 1961, with *Tiffany & C⁰ Private Stock*, and artist, *SC*. The name of this pattern is *Cirque de Pekin*. This cup and saucer are painted with bright colors in a very detailed chinoiserie motif of dragons and people. The quality of the painting and the design is exquisite. There are several other photographs of different pieces in this same pattern throughout the book. $275-$300

Demitasse Cup/Saucer, cup, 2.4" high x 2.3" in diameter and saucer, 4.75" in diameter. Le Tallec decorating mark 3, and *HH* (1957), with *Tiffany & C⁰ Private Stock*, and artist, *GD*. The name of the pattern is *Grignan Blanc sur Porcelaine Anglaise avec Relief*. The decoration includes gold, which is etched and brushed as well as painted. $175-$200

Demitasse Cups/Saucers, cups, 2.25" high x 2.25" in diameter and saucers, 4.6" in diameter, Le Tallec decorating mark 3 and *DD*, 1955, with artist, *CLS*. The name of the pattern is *Oiseaux Modernes*. The stylized birds are an unusual decorating theme for the Le Tallec studio, which is better known for its interpretations of 18ᵗʰ and 19ᵗʰ century patterns. One set, $150-$225

Cup/Saucer, cup, 2.4" high and saucer, 4.75" in diameter, Artoria porcelain mark 1, c. 1990-present, and Alice & Charly decorating mark 2, c. 1999-present. The pattern is called *Mimosa*, and it is artist signed, *N. Inacio* (Nizète German) *2000*. As mentioned earlier, Ms. German is one of the top decorators currently working in Limoges. (See additional background information on Ms. German on page 148.) $170

Demitasse Cup/Saucer, cup, 2.25" high x 2.25" in diameter and saucer, 4.4" in diameter, Haviland & Co. porcelain mark I, 1894-1931, and Haviland & Co. decorating mark c in red, 1876-1878/1889-1931, with *DECORATED BY* in red over decorating mark. This set is decorated with bright vibrant colors. $40-$50

Cup/Saucer, cup, 2" high x 3.5" in diameter and saucer, 5.4" in diameter, Haviland & Co. porcelain mark I, 1894-1931, and Haviland & Co. decorating mark c in red, 1876-1878/1889-1931. This is an extensively decorated cup and saucer, with a liberal use of gold around all the edges and transfers extending throughout the inside of the cup. $55-$70

Cup/Saucer, cup, 1.75" high x 2.9" in diameter and saucer, 4.4" in diameter, Haviland & Co. porcelain mark H, 1888-1896, and overglaze, *HAVILAND & C^O for WRIGHT KAY & C^O/DETROIT*. Yellow was not frequently used as a background color for Haviland china. The blue accents and the liberal use of gold accents make this set very striking. $75-$90

Right: Cup/Saucer, cup, 2.25" high x 3.5" in diameter and saucer, 5.75" in diameter, Tressemanes & Vogt porcelain mark 10, 1892-1907. This set is opulently decorated with blue enamel raised dots and gold filigree on the outside of the cup and the saucer. The inside of the cup and the handle are painted solid gold. This set was probably decorated by a European studio; it does not look like in was decorated in the U.S. $75-$95

Pedestal Cup/Saucer, cup, 2.4" high x 3.5" in diameter and saucer, 5.5" in diameter, Ahrenfeldt porcelain mark 7, c. 1896 and after, and marked, *FABRIQUE EN FRANCE/RICHARD BRIGGS CO./BOSTON/PATENTED*, with a fleur-de-lis in gold. The delicate handle complements the delicate pedestal shape of the cup. The flowers are hand painted and the gold filigree is transfers. $50-$60

Pedestal Cups/Saucers, cups, 3.6" to top of handle x 3" in diameter and saucers, 5.4" in diameter, Le Tallec decorating mark 3 and *HH*, 1957, with artist, *HD*. The name of the pattern is *Attributs Musique Or*. These cups, in the First Empire style, are decorated with gold work etched with an agate stone to give the design texture. $200+

Demitasse Cup/Saucer, cup, 2.25" high x 2.75" in diameter and saucer, 4.5" in diameter, Goumot-Labesse decorating mark 2 with *(RLV)* in black, from 1977. The pale, almost monochromatic, color of the transfer is what makes this a beautiful set. The transfer is enhanced with white enamel. $40-$50

Demitasse Cup/Saucer, cup, 2.5" high x 2.5" in diameter and saucer 5.25" in diameter, Limoges Castel porcelain mark 2, 1955-1979+, and Limoges decorating mark 19 in red. This is a typical souvenir set with a transfer of the Eiffel Tower. Companies in Limoges now produce a wide variety of items for tourists, and this is one of the better examples. $15-$20

Limoges Specialty Pieces

Figural Lamp, 13" high, Limoges porcelain mark 1. This lamp of a subdued Arabian-like couple represents the experimentation with an Oriental style. This piece is photographed in the Mannoni book (see Bibliography), which gives it a date of 1925. This is one of the nicest lamps we have seen from this period. $1,000-$1,200

Figural Lamp, 6.75" high x 4.6" wide x 5.5" deep. Other mark 2, used in the 1920s. Although the porcelain mark is partially illegible (but is definitely a Limoges mark), we are certain that this lamp was made in the 1920s. We base this dating on similar lamps, which were produced in Limoges about this time. This lamp, like most other figural lamps of this period, is entirely hand painted and has only a factory porcelain mark; however, these lamps were definitely factory decorated. Many of these lamps are also cracked from the heat of the light bulb, which probably happened because the original bulbs were replaced with ones with much higher wattage. These lamps are scarce. $500-$700

Left: Robert E. Lee Flask, 10.9" high, Georges Boyer decorating mark 3 in gold, from 1953. This flask could not be purchased by the public; it was given to distributors by the Southern Comfort company as a sales reward. $100

Nightlight, 10" high, Tharaud porcelain mark 1 in green, 1920-1945, and Tharaud decorating mark 2 in blue. This nightlight is a Spanish flamenco dancer with a mantilla. This nightlight reflects Tharaud's experimental decorating technique. Tharaud nightlights are highly collectible in Europe but are largely unknown to collectors in the U.S. These nightlights are quite rare. $1,000-$1,300

Decanter Set in Box, flask, 6.75" high x 4.4" deep x 1.5" wide and cups, 1.75" high x 1.5" square at top, Limoges Castel decorating mark 3 in gold and red, in use in 1979. These are the same blanks as the pieces in the decanter set below. This set is decorated with a large eagle and golden bees, which are associated with Napoleon. Note that some of the cups are still in their original paper wrappings. Complete set with box, $160 $200

Decanter Set, flask, 6.75" high x 4.4" deep x 1.5" wide and cups, 1.75" h x 1.5" square at top, Limoges Castel decorating mark 1 in green, 1944-1973, and Limoges Castel decorating mark 3 in green and gold, in use in 1979. It is rare to find a complete decanter set with all the pieces and in the original box. The decanter is nicely decorated with grape leaves on the front and a gold fleur-de-lis on the back. The cups have grape leaves on the front and fleurs-de-lis in gold on three sides. The stopper is in the shape of a feather. On the front of the decanter it reads, *La treille du Roy* (the royal grape vine). Complete set with box, $160-$200

Figural Liquor Bottles, 4.5" high, Limoges porcelain mark 2 in orange and overglaze mark in green, *Garnier/France*. The complete set, called "Skittles," includes six liquor bottles, which came in a box and were imported into the U.S. between 1935-1939. A small shipment was also imported in 1946. They were designed by a cousin of M. Garnier for Garnier Liqueurs. (See *A Guide to Miniature Bottles* in Bibliography.) The nurse is considered the hardest and the chef the easiest of the six bottles to find. These bottles are highly collectible by both Limoges and miniature bottle collectors. Set of six, $300+

Nurse   Chef

Clown   Bellboy   Sailor   Snowman

Robj

Robj was a retail store in Paris from 1921-1931. Robj sponsored annual design competitions from the late 1920s until 1931. Robj commissioned small decorative pieces in porcelain, mostly in art deco, for sale in the firm's Paris showroom, especially lamps, bottles and incense burners often in the form of human figures (see Elisabeth Cameron in Bibliography). These art deco flasks are scarce and highly sought after. We know that some, if not all, of these flasks were made by L. Michelaud in Limoges and other Limoges companies (see d'Albis & Romanet and Brega in Bibliography). The titles of these flasks are taken from the Brega book on Robj (see Bibliography).

Left: Prunelle, 10" high, Robj mark 1. Brega also identifies this piece as being made in Limoges. The figure is dressed in an *Alsacienne* (Alsace-Lorraine) costume. The word, "prunelle," means any of a variety of wild plums, which indicates that this bottle held a plum based liqueur. Robj flasks that are decorated with gold on white are scarcer than those decorated with other colors. $400+

Raspail, 10" high, Robj mark 1. According to d'Albis, this flask was made by Michelaud in Limoges. Although this flask is commonly referred to as the "Englishman," Raspail was actually a French chemist and politician who died in 1878. A famous boulevard in Paris is named after him. $400+

Rhum, 10.5" high, Robj mark 1. According to Brega, this flask was made in Limoges. "Rhum" is the French word for rum. This flask represents the inhabitants of Martinique, a former French colony, which was the main export source of rum imported into France. This piece appeared in the 1928 Robj catalogue. $500+

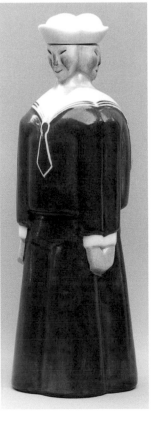

Right: Les Trois Matelots (Three Headed Sailor), 11" high Robj mark 1. This flask is in high demand by collectors. $1,200+

Left: Vieux Marc de Champagne (Old Mark from Champagne), 10" high, Robj mark 1. This piece is commonly referred to as the "Professor." The flask likely held a kind of champagne. $400+

Benedictine Monk, 10.25" high, Robj mark 1. Brega identifies this flask as being made in Limoges and notes that it was in the 1928 Robj catalogue. This flask held benedictine liqueur, which was made by the Benedictine monks. $400+

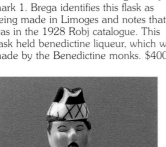

Right: La Cantiniere, 12" high, Robj mark 1. "La Cantiniere" is the name for a pretty young lady who cooks for soldiers—a camp waitress. $625+

Fine Napoleon, 10.25" high, Robj mark 2 in blue. This is a different Robj mark from the other flasks. Some of these flasks have a *Limoges/France* greenware mark and some do not, which indicates they were all made by a Limoges company. This flask appeared in the 1928 Robj catalogue. $400+

Left: Joueur de Cornemuse (Bagpipe Player), 10" high, Robj mark 1. Although commonly referred to as the "Scotsman," a "cornemuse" is a bagpipe like those used in Brittany in Northern France, where the men wore black round hats and bloused knickers. Brega states that this piece is a smaller model of Le Seyeux. $400+

Clown Cruet, 8.5" high, Robj mark 1, in black. This piece is very difficult to find. Note how the shape of the clowns contributes to the overall mood and that one clown is black and the other white. This piece was probably also made in Limoges. $1,500-$2,000.

Right: Untitled Flask, 10.5" high, Robj decorating mark 2. Brega did not title this flask or identify the type of liquor it held. Robj flasks decorated with only gold highlights are rarer than ones that are completely painted. $500-$650

Above left: Curaçao, 10.25" high, Robj decorating mark 1. This flask was pictured in the 1928 Robj catalogue. Commonly called the "Dutchman," this figure was a flask for curaçao liqueur, which is made from the dried peel of green oranges, which are grown and distilled in Curaçao, the largest of the Leeward Islands and of the Netherlands Antilles in the Caribbean Sea. The name, "Dutchman," then comes from the Dutch island of Curaçao. $500-$650

Left: Flask, 9.75" high, Michelaud decorating mark 2 in blue, after 1918, and marked on back, *Tangerine liqueur by Roger fils of Bordeausc.* This flask is nearly identical to the Robj flask (1929), *Guignolet*—an aperitif made with black cherries (*guignes*), and is further evidence that all of the Robj flasks were made in Limoges, and probably by Michelaud. $150-$200

Elephant Humidor, 7.25" high x 6.6" wide x 7" deep, Haviland & Co. porcelain mark A impressed, 1855—. These pieces are very rare, with probably only four or five known to exist. $10,000+

Ram Bookends, 5" high x 5.75" x 2.5", Tharaud porcelain mark 1.1 in green and Tharaud decorating mark 2 in blue. These pieces were made c. 1927-1930. These bookends reflect Tharaud's experimental decorating technique. Tharaud bookends are highly collectible in Europe but are largely unknown to collectors in the U.S. $500-$750

Cachepot, 7" high x 9.5" handle to handle, Le Tallec decorating mark 3 and *LL*, 1959, and artist, *jj*. The name of the pattern is *Cartels Fleurs Fond Pourpré Renceaux Or*. The hand painted floral pattern is very well decorated. $800+

Above Right: Clock, 13.25" high, Tressemanes & Vogt porcelain mark 8, 1892-1907, with *Ovington Bros./France* in red. Other Ovington Brothers marks also have the cities London, New York, or Chicago. Ovington Brothers was in business probably from the 1870s to sometime during the first half of the 20th century. The company both purchased decorated pieces from the various Limoges companies as well as decorated pieces themselves. Based on the quality of the decoration of this clock, we believe it was probably decorated by Ovington. Also, oftentimes pieces decorated by Limoges companies are marked on the back, *for Ovington Bros.* This piece is an excellent example of decoration, in this case gold highlights, which accentuates the patterns in the porcelain itself. The clockworks on this piece are original with the words, *New Haven/USA*, on the face. Limoges clocks are rare and the quality of decoration of this piece is even more rare. $1,000+

Horse Figurines, 4.1" high, Limoges Castel decorating mark 1, 1944-1973. Limoges Castel made several figurines, which are white with tan accents to provide definition. We have seen one other of these figurines of a lady holding a fan. Minimal use of decoration on predominately white objects is an interesting decorating technique. $30-$50

Mephistopheles Humidor, 8" high, Haviland &Co. porcelain mark A impressed, 1855—. Like the elephant humidor, this humidor is also very rare, with probably only four or five known to exist. $10,000+

Dresser Bottles, 6.75" high, 6" high, 4.5" high, and 4.75" high respectively, Le Tallec decorating mark 3 and *T*, 1950, with artist, *GK*. This pattern could not be identified by Le Tallec. We believe that these are dresser bottles, but in any case they are uncommon blanks. The chinoiserie motif includes four different scenes on each of the four pieces. The red borders and tops are also intricately decorated with gold highlights. These pieces are entirely hand painted. $2,000+

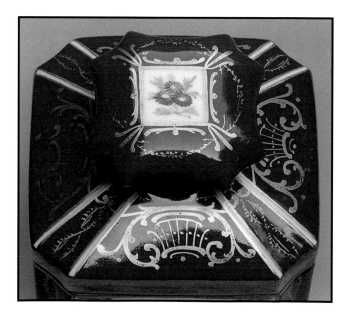

111

Left: Elephant Handle Box, 4.5" high x 4.25" x 4.25", Le Tallec decorating mark 3 and π or τ, 1974 or 1975, with *Tiffany & C° Private Stock*, and artist, *AM*. The name of the pattern is *Cirque de Pekin*. There are several other examples of this same pattern throughout the book. $650-$700

Dresser Tray, 15.5" x 12.5", Sazerat porcelain mark 1, 1852-1891, and Sazerat decorating mark 2 in red, 1852-1891. This piece is decorated with simple muted floral transfers, but the blank has an unusual shape. $100-$125

Washbasin and Pitcher, pitcher, 12" high and basin, 15.75" in diameter x 5.5" high, Demartial porcelain mark 2, 1883-1893. Like several Demartial pieces that we have seen, this set does not have a decorating mark but is definitely factory decorated. It is likely that these unmarked pieces were decorated during the early part of the firm's history. Pitchers and washbasins are difficult to find as a set because most of them were broken during use. A complete set would often include a soap dish, toothbrush holder, and chamber pot. $700-$800

Dresser Box, 3.5" high x 3.5" x 7.75", Redon porcelain mark 5, 1891-1896, and Redon decorating mark 3 in red, 1882-1896. This is an exquisite dresser box, both in terms of the decoration and the shape of the porcelain blank. The decoration complements and enhances the pattern in the porcelain, and it is entirely hand painted. $300-$375

Right & below: Candlesticks, 6.25" high, Le Tallec decorating mark 3 and *DD*, 1998, with artist, *VD*. The name of the pattern is *Laque de Chine*. The decoration on this set of candlesticks is exquisite and very detailed, with etched gold accents and Chinese figures framed in floral scenes. Pair, $1,800-$2,000

Three-Legged Dresser Box, 5.6" handle to handle, Gérard, Dufraisseix & Abbot porcelain mark 1, 1900-1953, and Gérard, Dufraisseix & Abbot decorating mark 5 in red, 1900-1941. Although this is a well designed blank, the decoration does not fit the blank. The piece has a shell finial; a sea motif would be more appropriate. $65-$85

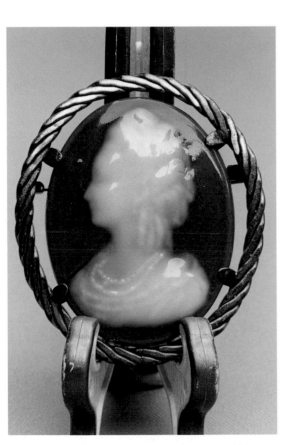

Broach, 2" x 1.4", Tharaud, mark 1 impressed, 1920-1945. This broach is a fine example of Tharaud's early work in relief and blue color fired under high temperatures under the glaze. $175-$225

Lighter and Ashtray, lighter, 4.9" high and ashtray, 5.25" x 3.1", Le Tallec decorating mark 3 and *WW*, 1965, with artist, *AD*. The name of the pattern is *Marin with Noir*. Cigarette lighters are difficult to find, and the use of the delicate gold lacing for part of the edging sets off the bolder black and gold design. $450-$525

Mask, 6.75" high x 6.75" wide, Limoges Castel decorating mark 1, 1944-1973. This is a portrait of Napoleon 1st. Made with a minimum of decoration, the mask is almost "alive" as a result of the "piercing" effect of the eyes. $50-$75

Candlestick Holder, 4.25" x 2.25", Bernardaud mark 7, current. $25-$35

Chamber Candlestick Holder, 3.24" in diameter, Gérard, Dufraisseix porcelain mark 1, 1890-1900. Although there is no decorating mark, this piece was factory decorated. These pieces are difficult to find. $75-$125

Display Signs. This is a sample of display signs used by several Limoges companies. Most of them incorporate the company's logo. Each, $40-$75

Chamber Candlestick Holder, 4" x 3.4", Gérard, Dufraisseix porcelain mark 1, 1890-1900, and Gérard, Dufraisseix decorating mark 2 in red, 1890-1900. This leaf shaped blank is very appealing, with the under tray extended to form the handle. $100-$150

Haviland Commemorative, 4.25" in diameter, T. Haviland porcelain mark R, 1962—, with *Haviland/Limoges/France* in gold. This commemorative dish is decorated with the Haviland logo and the dates, *1842-1967*, in gold. $25-$50

Frog Ashtray. 7.1" x 4.25". Bawo & Dotter decorating mark 4 in red, 1891-1896. We believe that both the frog and the lily pad are two separate ashtrays; and when not in use, the frog sits on the lily pad. These two blanks are unique and represent creativity in design and use. Both pieces are entirely hand painted. $175-$250

Haviland Commemorative. 2.6" in diameter. This commemorative seal in porcelain was issued in 1992 to mark the 150th anniversary of the Haviland companies. It reads, *SPETRI DE HAVILANT*, and includes the Haviland logo in the center. This seal comes in a blue felt pouch and was distributed to dealers. $60-$80

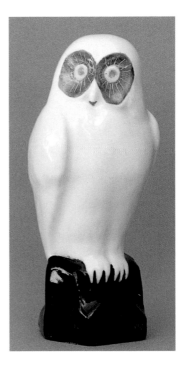

Owl Figurine. 4.75" high. Chamart decorating mark 2. Hand painted pieces with this mark date from the late 1960s through the 1970s, according to Leny Davidson, the president of Chamart. The blank and the decoration are simple and understated. $50+

Paris Embassy Ashtray. 4.4" x 3". T. Haviland porcelain mark R. 1962—. This ashtray is decorated with the Great Seal of the United States and the words, *American Embassy/ Paris*, in gold. $25-$45

Fox Figurine. 3" high x 6.9" x 4.5". Lanternier decorating mark 7. 1914-present. These figurines are scarce. Note how the shape of the porcelain almost gives life to the fox. This piece is a reminder of the pieces by E. Sandoz and was probably made around the same period, c. 1915-1920s. $275-$300

Mary Relief Portrait. 4.1" in diameter. AB Limoges mark 1 impressed on front of plaque and no mark on back. The words, *Ave Maria* (Hail Mary), are over the relief portrait of Mary. This piece could possibly have been a souvenir item sold in churches and stores selling religious material. The relief portrait is exceptionally detailed. $75+

Sculptures of d'Édouard Marcel Sandoz (1881-1971) for T. Haviland

Sandoz was a famous art deco sculptor who used many media for his sculptures—porcelain, bronze, marble, wood and crystal. All of the pieces shown here, unless otherwise noted in the captions, have the following marks: T. Haviland porcelain mark M impressed, 1894-1957, and T. Haviland decorating mark p, 1903-1924, with the words, *COPYRIGHT* and *DÉPOSÉ*, and signed, *E. M. Sandoz SC*, and impressed, *ESZ*. Some of the original Sandoz pieces were reproduced in the 1970s, but these pieces are marked differently. Also, the colors of these reproductions are much bolder than the originals.

Frog Flower Vase, 7.1" high, in 1916 catalogue and available in several colors and three sizes. $700+

Right: White Frog Bank or Cardholder, 4" high. T. Haviland porcelain mark M impressed and *ESZ* impressed only, in 1916 catalogue and available in several colors and only one size. Sandoz created this sculpture to symbolize his appetite for Paris when he first arrived there about 10 years earlier. $400-$550

Left: Frog Flower Vase, 6" high, in 1916 catalogue and available in several colors and three sizes. $400-$550

Kingfisher on a Shell, 5" high x 8" x 6.25", in 1917 catalogue and available in several colors and three sizes. This is one of the best-decorated Kingfishers on a Shell that we have seen. The blues and greens run together into white on the shell, and the feathers are painted with striking blue and green stripes. $700-$900

Mandarin Duck Bonbon, 6.25" long x 3" high, in 1916 catalogue and available in several colors and several sizes. This shape also came in two smaller sizes to be used as mustards. $350-$450

Monkey Tobacco Jar, 6" high. $700-$800

Baby Milk Bottle Jar, 9.6" high, T. Haviland porcelain mark M impressed and *ESZ* impressed, available in 1916 catalogue in several colors and three sizes. $800+

Monkey Tobacco Jar, 7" high, in 1916 catalogue and available in several colors and three sizes. $700-$800

Monkey Tobacco Jar, 8.5" high. $700-$800

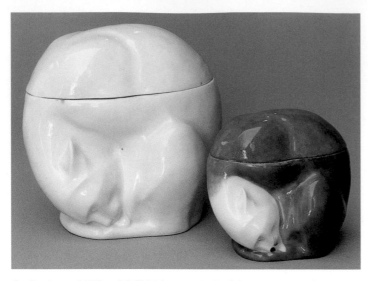

Cat Bonbons, 6.75" and 4.6" high respectively, did not appear in the catalogue but were made in 1916 and were available in several colors and four sizes. These two pieces also have the T. Haviland porcelain mark O, 1920-1936. Large cat, $700-$800 and small cat, $500-$600

Desert Fox Bonbon, 4.7" high and 7" ear to ear, not in catalogue but in 1921 list of Sandoz pieces and available in several colors and four sizes. $800-$900

Parakeet Pitcher, 7" high and 9.75" from beak to tail, in 1916 catalogue and available in several colors and only one size. $650-$800

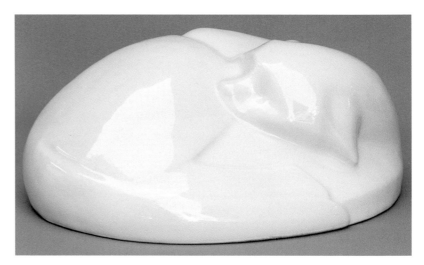

Cat Foot Warmer, 3.9" high x 9.75" x 7.75", *ESZ* impressed, a rare blank produced in 1916 and available in more than one size. $800+

Duck Pitchers, 6.25" and 5.1" high respectively, in 1916 catalogue and available in several colors and three sizes. Large duck, $450-$500 and small duck, $300-$375

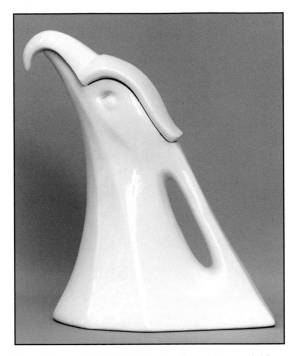

Eagle Pitcher, 9.75" high, T. Haviland porcelain mark M impressed and ESZ impressed, available in 1916 catalogue and available in several colors and one size. $800+

Cat Flasks, 12", 8.6", and 7.25" high respectively, in 1916 catalogue and available in several colors and four sizes. Large cat, $550-$650 and small cat, $450-$500

Cups, 2.4" high x 2.5" in diameter. These cups also have the T. Haviland porcelain mark O, 1920-1936. Each, $85-$95

Tea Set, teapot, 5" high; tray, 10.5" wide x 5" deep; and cups, 1.25" high x 2.75" in diameter, in 1916 catalogue and teapot available in three sizes. $1,200-$1,500

Knife Rest, 1.75" high x 5", in 1916 catalogue and available in several colors and two sizes. $250-$300

Mushroom and Frog Salt Cellars, both in 1916 catalogue, mushroom available in several colors and four sizes and frog available in several colors and one size. Pair, $300-$350

Two Frog Salt Cellars, pink frog on left is an original signed Sandoz piece and the maroon frog on the right is a reproduction, with *044/1000, HAVILAND/LIMOGES/FRANCE* in blue. Note the much brighter and deeper color of the reproduction piece. Original frog, $125-$175 and reproduction frog, $50-$75

Right: Cockatoo, 21.75" high, only marks are T. Haviland porcelain mark Q, 1946-1962, and *ESZ* impressed. The cockatoo did not appear in the catalogue, but it was first produced in small numbers in 1925. After World War II, larger numbers of them were made until 1984. There are two sizes, and the colors are ivory and white and some have highlighted colors on their feet and eyes. $3,000+

Below: Gosling Pitcher, 6.25" high, in 1916 catalogue and available in *several* colors and two sizes. $550-$650

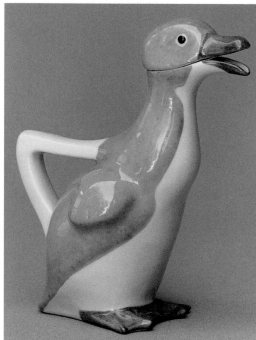

Gosling Cruets, 6.75" high, in 1917 catalogue and available in several colors and only one size. $650-$700

Left: Cockatoo, 14.5" high, T. Haviland porcelain mark R, 1962—, and *ESZ* impressed. This cockatoo is the smaller of the two sizes. See accompanying caption under Cockatoo on previous page. $1,000-$1,200

Right: Fish Vase (*Poisson de Chine*), 7.6" high, T. Haviland porcelain mark M impressed and *ESZ* impressed, in 1917 catalogue and available in several colors and one size. The white blank emphasizes the sculpted shape of the vase. $500+

Fish Vase, 9.75" high, T. Haviland porcelain mark M impressed, 1894-1957, and T. Haviland decorating mark t in blue, 1967—, with *hand painted from a design of E. Sandoz/edition limitée no: 040/ 1000* in blue. This is a reproduction of an original Sandoz piece, which appeared in the 1917 catalogue. Note the much brighter and deeper color. $150-$175

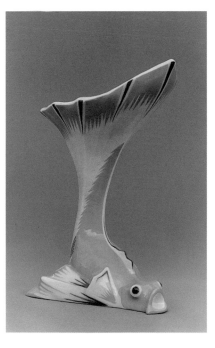

Gosling Pitcher, 7" high. Most of these pitchers do not have the painted black accents like this one. $600-$700.

Undecorated Limoges Blanks

"Goose" Girl, 11.5" high, *Joe Descomps* and *Limoges* impressed. Joe Descomps, 1869-1950, was a sculptor of mostly bronze and bronze and ivory figures. This is the only Joe Descomps sculpture in Limoges porcelain that we have seen. The sculpture conveys a mood of playfulness, and the porcelain is very detailed. $700+

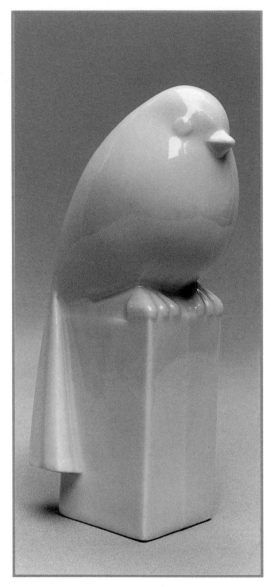

Bird Figurine, 6" high, Gérard, Dufraisseix, Abbot porcelain mark 6, 1900-1953. This sparrow is representative of the cubist art movement in the early part of the 20th century. This is a very special piece, which is in the Royal Limoges collection and has been photographed in the Mannoni book (see Bibliography). The porcelain is ivory colored, and it was not meant to be decorated. $500+

Arabian Couple, 11" high. Although not marked, this figurine is definitely made by a Limoges factory. It is the same blank, only smaller, as the lamp on page 104. Like the lamp, this blank shows an Asian influence in the design, which was popular in Limoges figurine lamps during the 1920s. $300-$400.

Candlestick, 8.5" high, Coiffe porcelain mark 2, c. 1891-c. 1914. This candlestick is very ornately designed. Pieces like this are quite rare. $75-$100

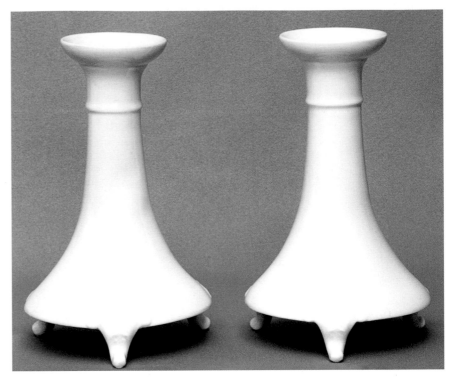

Pair of Candlesticks, 6" high, Porcelaine Limousine porcelain mark 1, 1906-1938. These candlesticks have simple curved "Queen Anne style" feet, which complement the simple shape of the candlesticks themselves. Pair, $100-$150

Above: Dove, 4.75" high x 9" from beak to tail, Limoges mark 1, date unknown but probably produced sometime after 1950. There are identical doves in different sizes, and ones that are similar, which are name card holders, but they are much smaller. Note the texture of the feathers. The dove has its wings partially extended as if ready to begin flight. $40-$50

Left: Seashell, 7.5" high x 8.75" diagonal, Bernardaud porcelain mark 3, 1900-1978, with *Primavera/France* in an overglaze rectangle. This is an undecorated piece, which portrays the perfect form of a natural seashell. This piece was not intended for decoration and has no function other than an art object. $75-$100

Celadon Duck, 10.5" high, Chamart decorating mark 1, up to c. 1985. According to Leny Davidson, president of Chamart, both a celadon and a white duck were made in the 1980s. The celadon coloring is in the porcelain, not in the enamel glaze. The duck is very lifelike and holds its wings partially extended. The pattern of the feathers on the porcelain is very detailed. $150-$225

Owl, 7.5" high, Limoges porcelain mark 1. The design of this piece portrays the owl's strength as a bird of prey. The feathers are much coarser than those on the duck and the dove. $100-$150

Lion Cub Figurine, 2.25" high x 3.75" nose to tail, Tharaud porcelain mark 1.1, 1920-1945, and Tharaud decorating mark 2 in blue, 1920-1945. The Millon and Robert auction in 1995 (see Bibliography) featured several Camille Tharaud animal figurines, which commanded high prices. This figurine is one of Tharaud's "connoisseur" pieces. The lion cub has a unique glaze pattern on top of his head, which looks like lion cub fur. $275-$300

Turtle Box, 2.5" high x 5" long x 4" wide, Chamart decorating mark 2, late 1960s-current. The pattern of the porcelain on the back of the turtle is quite detailed, and the turtle is in "slow" motion. The shell is the lid of the box. Unhinged boxes of animals of this size are not common. $55-$65

Bird Napkin Holder, 3.25" high x 5.75" wide, T. Haviland porcelain mark R, 1962—. $20-$30

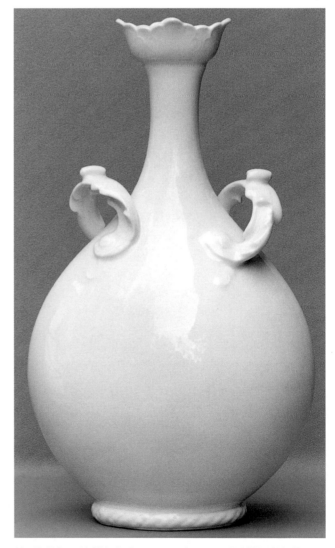

Bud Vase, 4.4" high, Bawo & Dotter decorating mark 4 in red, 1891-1896. Although there is a decorating mark on this vase, there is no decoration, which is very unusual. Also, there are no outlines or other visible signs that any decoration was removed. After the failure of the Bawo & Dotter firm in 1915, about $350,000 of its goods were purchased at auction by George Borgfeldt & Co. What seems likely is that the decorating mark was applied to pieces waiting to be decorated when the firm went out of business, and these pieces were subsequently bought and sold as blanks by Borgfeldt. To support this conjecture, we have had suspicions about some decorated pieces with this same Bawo & Dotter decorating mark. These pieces appear to be decorated by amateur painters and not by the Bawo & Dotter factory. The pattern that circles the top part of this vase and the jagged bud openings contrast nicely with the smooth surface of the main body of the vase. $75-$85

Handled Vase, 11.5" high, Pouyat porcelain mark 7, 1891-1932. This was a very popular blank, which was widely painted by amateur U.S. artists. The blank is more interesting than most of the amateur decorated pieces. $170-$200

Pitcher, 8.9" high, Haviland & Co. porcelain mark F, 1876-1889. The braided rope handle, which divides at the top, is an attractive feature of this blank. $175-$200

Handled Vase, 7" high, Limoges mark 0.5, before 1891 and *DEPOSÉ* impressed. This blank is unusual. $75-$125

Sugar, 6.75" high, Haviland & Co. porcelain mark F, 1876-1889. The seashell finial and the handles are well shaped and delicate. $75-$80

Dragonfly Tea Cup, 2" high x 3.5" in diameter, Guérin porcelain mark 4, 1891-1932. This three-footed cup is well designed with a dragonfly handle, which is reminiscent of the Haviland & Co. butterfly handled cups. This cup also comes in a demitasse size. $75-$90

Pitcher, 8.5" high, Haviland & Co. porcelain mark D, 1876-1886. This piece has a raised design around the handle—a nautical theme of an anchor with a cable handle. $85-$100

Gravy with Attached Underplate, 3" high x 7" x 6.5", Haviland & Co. porcelain mark H, 1888-1896. This gravy in the Marseilles blank gives this piece an almost "cabbage"-like effect. The handle is designed as a swirl of porcelain. This is a striking blank. $100-$125

Leaf Dish, 6" x 6.75", Haviland & Co. porcelain mark I, 1894-1931. This is a well designed blank, which shows the veins of the leaf. $45-$50

Oyster Cup, 1" high x 2.9" x 3.25", Délinières porcelain mark 2, 1891-1900. Note that the blank and the ridges on the underside are shaped like an oyster. There is a decorated example of this same oyster cup on page 40. $75-$85

Invalid Feeder, 3.1" high x 6.75" long, C. F. Haviland porcelain mark 2 impressed, c. 1865-1881, and Gérard, Dufraisseix & Morel porcelain mark 1, 1881-1890. This is one of the more interesting invalid feeder blanks because, unlike most them, there is a pattern in the porcelain. Invalid feeders are not common. $85-$125

Oyster Plate, 8.25" square, Gérard, Dufraisseix & Morel porcelain mark 1, 1881-1890. The pattern of the blank of this oyster plate is very intricate, and the porcelain itself is very heavy. If this plate were hand painted to enhance the pattern of the blank, the painting would half to be very detailed. $125-$150

Paris by Night Candleholder, 2.75" high x 4.5" in diameter, Bernardaud mark 8, current. Bernardaud produced a series of these domed candleholders, called VotiveLights™, each with a separate theme. The one pictured here is of Paris by Night. Others include, for example, New York, London, and Disney World. When lit with a candle, the objects in the porcelain are highlighted. The beauty of the decoration of these pieces is in the cluster of images, which let out varying shades of light. $45-$55

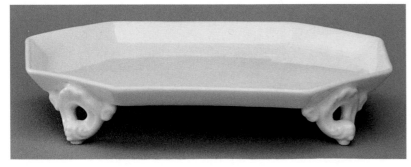

Footed Soap Dish, 1" high x 5.25" x 3.6", Tressemanes & Vogt porcelain mark 10, 1892-1907. This is a scarce blank. The simple tray contrasts with the ornate feet. $60-$80

Vanity Jar, 3.1" high x 4.25" in diameter, Limoges Castel porcelain mark 2, 1955-1979+. With the scalloped design in the porcelain, this piece is attractive as a white blank; or it could be decorated with highlights that emphasize the scalloped pattern in the porcelain. $50-$60

Dresser Vanity Jar, 2.5" high x 4.5" in diameter, Bawo & Dotter decorating mark 4 in red, 1891-1896. As with the earlier white bud vase, this vanity jar has a decorating mark with no decoration, and there is no evidence that any previous decoration has been removed. See the earlier comments about the bud vase, and the failure of the Bawo & Dotter firm in 1915, which may explain how this occurred. This is a common blank that was used frequently by amateur decorators in the U.S. $40-$50

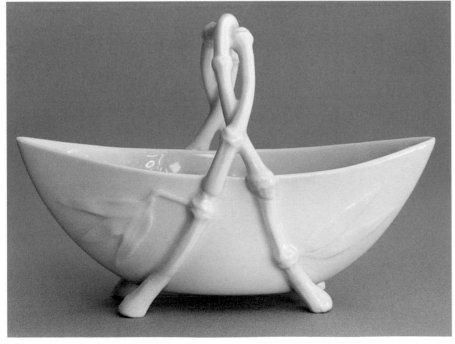

Bamboo Handled Basket, 4" high x 5.75" x 2.6", Limoges porcelain mark 3, date unknown. The foliage pattern in the boat shaped basket complements the applied bamboo handle, which is really the focus of this piece. The design is unusual. $70-$75

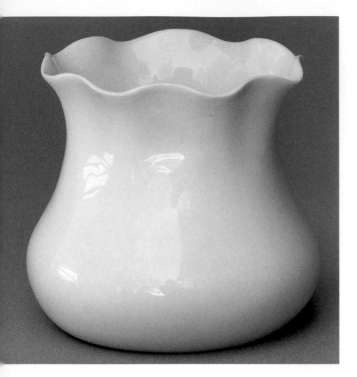

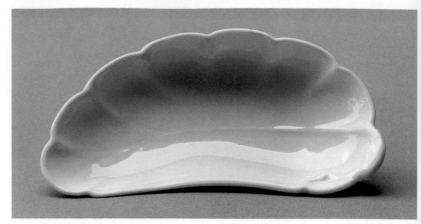

Above: Leaf Bone Dish, 6" x 3.5", Haviland & Co. porcelain mark H, 1876-1896. This is a simple but elegant bone dish in the shape of a leaf, with a center vein and outside ridges. $20-$25

Left: Fluted "Vase," 4.5" high x 4.4" in diameter at the top, Gérard, Dufraisseix & Morel porcelain mark 1, 1881-1890. We are not sure of the purpose of this piece, but it is well-proportioned. $60-$75

Horse Head Ashtray, 4.9" high x 8.5" in diameter, T. Haviland porcelain mark Q, 1946-1962, and T. Haviland decorating mark s, 1958-1967. This distinctive piece is only produced as a white blank, as indicated by the T. Haviland decorating mark. The indentations for holding the cigarettes are in the shape of horseshoes, and the horse's head is reminiscent of those on a carousel. According to Nora Travis, this ashtray is listed in the 1967-68 Haviland catalogue under giftware as *Cheval Blanc* (white horse). $150-$175

Ashtray, 4.25" square, Fontanille & Marraud porcelain mark 4, used in 1979 and after. We like the detail in this blank. $15-$25

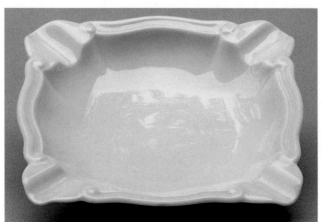

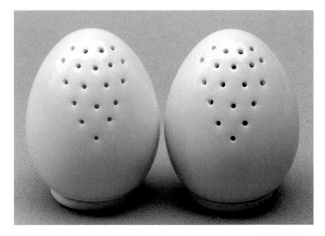

Salt and Pepper Shakers, 2.4" high, Giraud porcelain mark 2, 1920s-used in 1979. Egg-shaped, these shakers have the holes on the side. The design is simple and elegant. Set, $40-$60

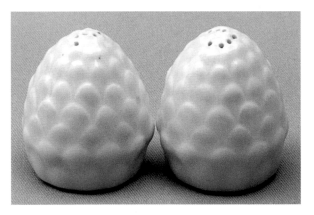

Salt and Pepper Shakers, 2" high, Limoges porcelain mark 1. The blanks for this set have a pine cone pattern. The holes in the tops are shaped into an S and P. These types of salt and pepper shakers are not atypical. Set, $30-50

Ice Relish, 1.6" high x 9.1" x 8.5", Haviland & Co. porcelain mark 1, 1894-1931. We have seen several decorated pieces on this blank; this undecorated one, however, is more attractive. $40-$50

Sugar Bowl, 5.6" high x 6.25" handle to handle, Haviland & Co. porcelain mark 1, 1894-1931. The curved handles and finial are the distinguishing characteristics of this well designed sugar bowl. $40-$50

Individual Coffee Set, tray, 11.4" x 8"; coffee pot, 6" high; sugar, 3" high; creamer, 1.75" high; and cups, 2.1" high x 2" in diameter and saucers, 4.4" in diameter. Lanternier porcelain mark 5, 1891-1914, on coffeepot and sugar, and Limoges porcelain mark 1 on creamer, tray and cups/saucers. Complete individual coffee sets are difficult to find. $200-$275

Right: Cup/Saucer, cup, 1.9" high x 3.5" in diameter and saucer, 5.5" in diameter, T. Haviland porcelain mark M impressed, 1894-1957, and T. Haviland decorating mark p in green, 1903-1925. It is unusual for a white dinnerware blank to have a T. Haviland decorating mark. Light shows through the body of the cup, which gives an effect similar to that of a star sapphire. The cup and saucer are beautifully molded, and much of the porcelain pattern is lost when the pieces are decorated, especially with floral designs. The Haviland pieces designed by Suzanne Lalique use this same blank; but because they are simply decorated, the effect of the pattern in the porcelain is still visible. $25-$40

Demitasse Cup/Saucer, cup, 2.5" high x 2.25" in diameter and saucer, 5" in diameter, Blondeau, Pichonnier & Duboucheron porcelain mark 1, 1891-1906. The saucer is exceptionally well designed with a wavy pattern divided into four sections. $25-$30

Bouillon Cup/Saucer, cups, 2" high x 3.5" in diameter and saucer, 5.5" in diameter, Haviland & Co. porcelain mark 1, 1894-1931. This cup and saucer in white represents an example of understated elegance, which is enhanced by the thinness and translucency of the porcelain. Set of eight, $200-$225

Bouillon Cup/Saucer, cup, 2" high x 3.6" in diameter and saucer, 5.9" in diameter, Bawo & Dotter porcelain mark 11, 1896-1920. The handles on this bouillon cup are both elegant and delicate. $25-$30.

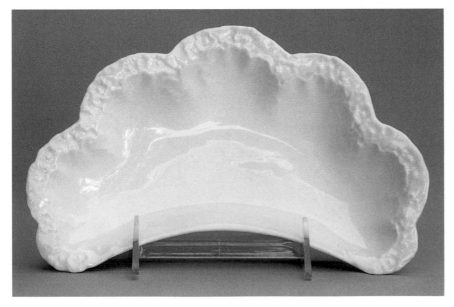

Salad Dish, 8.75" x 4.5", Lanternier porcelain mark 5, 1891-1914. This piece has an intricately patterned rim and the curved side is scalloped. $25-$30

Butter Dish, 3.75" high x 7.5" handle to handle, T. Haviland porcelain mark M impressed, 1894-1957, and T. Haviland porcelain mark L in brown, 1893. The design of this butter dish is odd, since the top and bottom appear to have different patterns; however, the T. Haviland brown mark is on both the top and the bottom of the butter set, and we have seen this piece with the same transfer pattern on the cover, liner and base. This piece is an example of a rather poor porcelain design, in terms of matching lid and base, which can best be seen on the white blank. $125-$150

Compote, 3.1" high x 9" in diameter, T. Haviland porcelain mark M in red, 1894-1957 and T. Haviland decorating mark p in red, 1903-1925. This piece has a well designed base. $75-$125

Sectional Dish, 11.25" x 9.5", C. F. Haviland porcelain mark 3, 1865-1881. This is a beautifully designed dish with ragged leaf shaped edges and with the bases at both ends of the handle forming half shell shaped curves. $175-$250

Relish Dish, 10" x 4", Pouyat porcelain mark 7, 1891-1932. From the wave shaped ends, edges, and outer pattern to the boat shaped bowl, this piece is extremely well designed. The entire piece suggests ocean waves. We have seen this piece decorated, but the beauty of the shape of the porcelain is diminished to a great extent. $75-$90

Tureen, 9.5" high x 13.5" x 8.25", Haviland & Co. porcelain mark B impressed, 1865-1876. This is a large, oval plain tureen offset with straight, sharply crossed handles. This piece is very striking. $200-$300

Covered Vegetable, 5" high x 9" handle to handle, Gérard, Dufraisseix & Morel porcelain mark 1, 1881-1890. This is a typical example of serving pieces manufactured during this period, and earlier, with raised designs around the handles. Often these designs or patterns were shaped as clusters of leaves. $60-$80

Cider Pitcher, 6" high x 8.5" from lip to end of handle, Tressemanes & Vogt porcelain mark 10, 1892-1907. Like the shaving mugs, very few examples of these pitchers have Limoges decorating marks; most were decorated in the U.S. $75-$125

Cachepot, 9.25" high, Guérin porcelain mark 4, 1891-1932. Most of the cachepots available in the U.S. are poorly decorated by amateur American painters. It is difficult to find a white blank. This blank is much more interesting as an undecorated piece. $125-$175

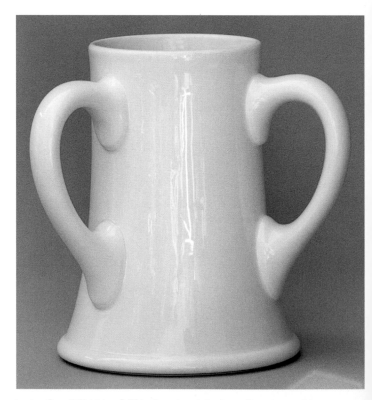

Loving Cup, 7.5" high x 5.7" in diameter at the base, Pouyat porcelain mark 7, 1891-1932. We have seen several examples of these cups decorated by professional U.S. studios and very few with Limoges decorating marks. There are also a large number that were decorated by amateur painters. Professionally decorated loving cups command relatively high prices. $125-$150

Shaving Mug, 3.6" high, Gérard, Dufraisseix, Abbot porcelain mark 6, 1900-1953. Very few examples of these mugs have Limoges decorating marks; most were decorated in the U.S. $25-$40

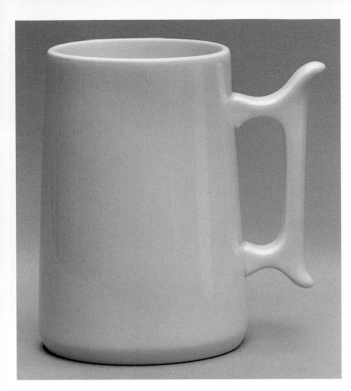

Left: Mug, 5.6" high, Tressemanes & Vogt porcelain mark 10, 1892-1907. Amateur U.S. painters decorated the majority of the available tankard sets—pitchers and mugs; however, there are quite a few examples of richly decorated sets by the Pickard and Stouffer studios. Very few sets have Limoges decorating marks. $35-$50

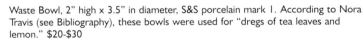

Waste Bowl, 2" high x 3.5" in diameter, S&S porcelain mark 1. According to Nora Travis (see Bibliography), these bowls were used for "dregs of tea leaves and lemon." $20-$30

Left: Cup, 2.5" high x 2.6" in diameter, Haviland & Co. porcelain mark H, 1888-1896. The purpose of this cup is unclear. The lip around the top makes it uncomfortable as a demitasse cup for drinking, and the porcelain is very heavy. In the Haviland & Co. catalogue titled, "Grand Prix Paris 1889," the blank is found on page 94, with the page titled, "Round Edge." There are three different sized cups with the same shape, and they are referred to as "Cups tub round edge." This is the only cup in this blank that we have seen. $40

Plaques, 11.1" x 8.9", 7.25" x 5", 3.9" x 3", 3.5" x 2.4", Limoges Castel porcelain mark 2, 1955-1979+. These pieces are obviously meant for decoration. Set of four, $275

Limoges Boxes

The photographs of Limoges boxes are organized by the companies that import them into the U.S., except for Le Tallec which is strictly a decorating studio. We have selected these seven companies, based upon the generally high quality of their boxes. Pieces decorated by Le Tallec in Paris and Alice & Charly, a relatively new decorating studio, in Limoges consistently set the highest standards in the quality of their decoration.

Le Tallec

Le Tallec Display Sign

All Le Tallec pieces are entirely hand painted.

Rectangle Box with Gold, 5.1" x 8.4", Limoges Castel porcelain mark 1, used in 1950-1979+, and Le Tallec decorating mark 3 and *UU*, 1964, with artist, *cc.* The name of the pattern is *Guirlande de Fleurs Or in Relief.* This is a simple hand painted hinged box with gold flowers and accents in relief. $250-$300

Unhinged Blue Accented, Floral Chinoiserie Box, 1.9" high x 5.25" x 3.5", Limoges Castel porcelain mark 2, used in 1950-1979+, and Le Tallec decorating mark 3 and probably σ, 1968, with *Tiffany & C° Private Stock*, and artist, *AC*. The name of the pattern is *Princesse de Chine*. $300-$350

Hinged Gold/Floral Egg Box, 3.75" high x 4.5" x 3", Le Tallec decorating mark 3 and ζ, 1969, with artist, *FG*. The name of the pattern is *Clairette Jaune*. This entirely hand painted piece is decorated with gold grapes with relief accents and strings of orange and yellow flowers. $300-$350

139

Hinged Floral Box, 2.5" high x 5.25" x 3.5", Limoges Castel mark 2, used in 1955-1979+, and Le Tallec decorating mark 3 and S, 1950, with *Tiffany & Cº Private Stock*, and artist, *FE*. The name of the pattern is *Fleurs Polychromes with Gris*. Large floral patterns are unusual on Le Tallec pieces. $200-$250

Unhinged Yellow Chinoiserie Box, 2" high x 4.25" x 3", Le Tallec decorating mark 3 and either *P* or ρ, 1948 or 1974, with *Tiffany & Cº Private Stock*, and artist, *GM*. This pattern could not be identified by Le Tallec. $225-$275

Hinged Rectangle Message Box, 1.25" high x 4" x 1.6", Le Tallec decorating mark 3 and probably θ, 1970, with *Tiffany & Cº Private Stock*, and artist, *MP*. The name of this pattern is *Ruban Rose et Bleuets*. On the top of the box are the words, *Between a Yes and No Ther's* [sic] *not room For a pin to go-*. $175-$225

Hinged Chinoiserie Scenic Box, 5.1" x 3.4", Limoges Castel porcelain mark 2, used in 1950-1979+, and Le Tallec decorating mark 3 and *DD*, 1955, with artist, *AG*. This pattern could not be identified by Le Tallec. $350-$400

Grape and Floral Hinged Box, 2.1" high x 2.1" in diameter, Le Tallec decorating mark 3 and *RO*, 1985, with artist, *PP*. The name of the pattern is *Clairette Bleu*. The grapes are painted with heavy gold and the flowers are accented with blue enameling. $300-$325

Grape and Floral Hinged Box, 2.1" high x 2.1" in diameter, Le Tallec decorating mark 3 and *RZ*, 1991, with artist, *SHF*. The name of the pattern is *Treille Muscate*. This box was made exclusively for Lucy Zahran, Beverly Hills, in a limited edition of 50. It was designed in honor of Camille Le Tallec's daughter. $325-$375

Figures and Dragons Chinoiserie Hinged Box, 2" high x 3.5" x 2.5", Le Tallec decorating mark 3 and π, 1974, with *Tiffany & C° Private Stock*, and artist, *AC*. The name of this pattern is *Cirque de Pekin*. This same pattern is shown elsewhere on other pieces. This is one of our favorite Le Tallec patterns, and the details of the painting of the figures and dragons are exquisite. $450-$550

Hinged Oval "Pinwheel" Box, 2" high x 3.5" wide, Le Tallec decorating mark 3 and *RP*, 1986, and *Tiffany & C° Private Stock*, with artist *VM*. The name of this pattern is *Alcyon*. The decoration on this box is so precise that it is very difficult to tell that it is totally hand painted. $450-$550

Right & below: Hinged Striped Box in Case, 4.5" x 1.9", Le Tallec decorating mark 3 and ζ, 1973, with artist, *AL*. The name of this pattern is *Grignan Bleu*. The gold is exquisitely painted with an unusual brushed effect on the gold bands. $350-$400

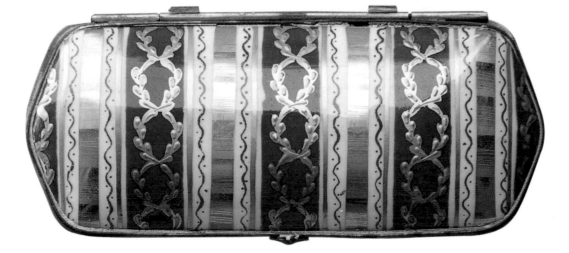

143

Hinged Egg Message Box, 2" high x 3.25" wide, Le Tallec decorating mark 3 and v, 1976, with *Tiffany & C° Private Stock*, and artist, *EG*. The name of this pattern is *Liseron Bande Jaune*. On the top of the box it reads, *The Friends Gift*. $250-$275

Hinged Blue and Orange Box, 5" high, Le Tallec decorating mark 3 and *VV*, 1964, with *specialment pour Bonwit Teller*, and artist, *JN*. The name of this pattern is *Nicoletta Rouge with Gris*. $300-$325

Right & below: Hinged Round Black and Gold Chinoiserie Box, 2" high and 4" in diameter, Le Tallec decorating mark 3 and *RE*, 1980, with artist, *VM*. The name of this pattern is *Nuit de Chine*. The hand painting on this box and the following tray are very close to the actual style of decoration in China and Japan. The unusual black background makes a striking contrast to the gold figures. $300-$400

Four Legged Chinoiserie Tray, 1.1" high x 6" x 4.5", Le Tallec decorating mark 3 and *RP*, 1986, with artist, *AO*. This pattern is the same as the previous box, *Nuit de Chine*. This tray, however, introduces silver paint that is used for the children's heads, arms, and legs. It is very difficult to find matching occasional Le Tallec pieces on the secondary market. $400-$500

Gold Chinoiserie Hinged Egg Box, 1.75" high x 3.4" x 2.1", Le Tallec decorating mark 3 and α, 1967, with artist, *JN*. The name of this pattern is *Oiseaux Graves Polychromes*. The gold is acid etched and the birds are brilliantly colored. $450-$600

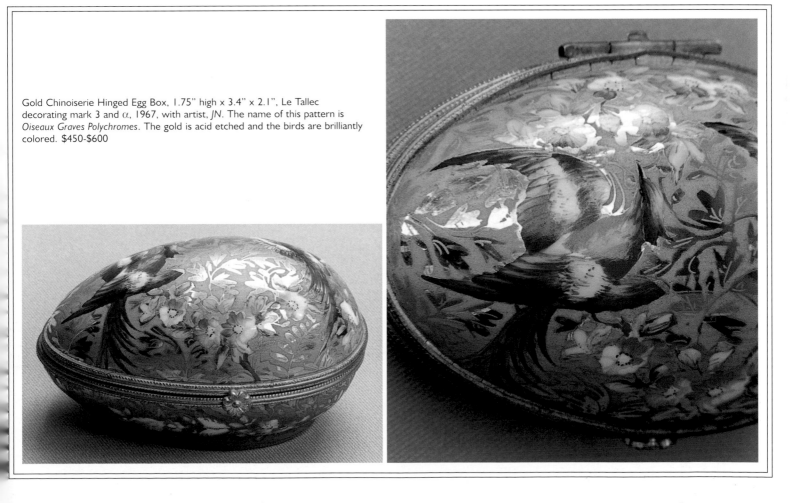

Fan with Golden Bird, 1.25" high x 2.75" x 2.6", Le Tallec decorating mark 3 and *DC*, 1997, with artist, *SP*. The name of the pattern is *Oiseaux Sèvres*, and the decoration is a combination of etched and painted gold. $175-$225

Heart Shaped Hinged Box, 3.5" at widest point, Le Tallec decorating mark 3 and *YY* , 1966, with artist, *AD*. The name of this pattern is *Marin with Pourpre*. The gold is painted in relief against a maroon background. The metal work on this box, as with all Le Tallec boxes, is very plain. $400-$500

Egg on Stand, 3" high on stand, marked, *Le Tallec á Paris/France*. The name of the pattern is *Luciolle Vertical*, and it first appeared in 1995. The decoration is a combination of brushed and etched gold. $225-$275

Bird of Paradise Box, 2.25" x 5.25" x 3.5", Le Tallec decorating mark 3 and *RF*, 1981, with artist, *JN*. The name of the pattern is *Cartels Oiseaux Polychrome Fond Vert Émeraude Marin Or.* $600-$650

Fox, 2" high x 2.25" in diameter, Le Tallec decorating mark 3 and *DD*, 1998, with artist, *CM*. Subject boxes, as opposed to traditional shaped boxes, are unusual for Le Tallec. The hand painting in just gold emphasizes the well shaped blank. $175

Egg, 2.75" high x 3.75" x 2.75", Le Tallec decorating mark 3 and *RW*, 1989, with *Tiffany & Co Private Stock*, and artist, *GP*. The name of the pattern is *Black Shoulder*. This is a very popular pattern. $350-$400

Elephant, 3.5" high, Le Tallec decorating mark 3 and *DD*, 1998, with artist, *CM*. Like the previous box, the all gold decoration emphasizes the well designed blank of an active elephant. $220

Floral Egg, 2.5" long, marked *Tiffany & Co*. See comments under Egg on Stand photo on next page. $125-$150.

Latticework Box, 5.25" wide x 3.6" deep, Le Tallec decorating mark 3 and *R?* (second letter is illegible but looks like a ? mark, decorated sometime between 1978-1991), with *Tiffany & C° Private Stock*, and artist, *GP*. The hand painted latticework is very detailed. $400+

Egg on Stand, egg. 2.5" high, marked *Tiffany & C°*. Although this box does not have the Le Tallec decorating mark, it is definitely decorated by Le Tallec. According to Laurence de La Grange, the manager of Le Tallec, the studio does not use the Le Tallec decorating mark on Tiffany eggs. Both the grapes and the vines are decorated with raised gold. The studio has not decorated any pieces with grapes within the last 15 years. $175-$225

S&D Limoges

The Cardinet Collection

The following several boxes are decorated by Nizète German, who heads the decorating company, Alice & Charly (the names of her two children), which was established in Limoges in 1995. S&D Limoges is the exclusive distributor of Alice and Charly decorated pieces in the U.S., and many of the designs are exclusive to S&D Limoges. Particularly inspired by 18th century motifs, many of the Alice & Charly designs are heavily accented with gold and platinum. Pieces are either signed *N. German* or *N. Inacio*. (See Alice & Charly decorating marks.) The previous signature was discontinued because some collectors mistook Ms. German's name to be the country of origin. *Inacio* is derived from Ms. German's maiden name, *Nacio*. Alice & Charly is one of the best decorators in Limoges.

S&D Limoges Display Sign

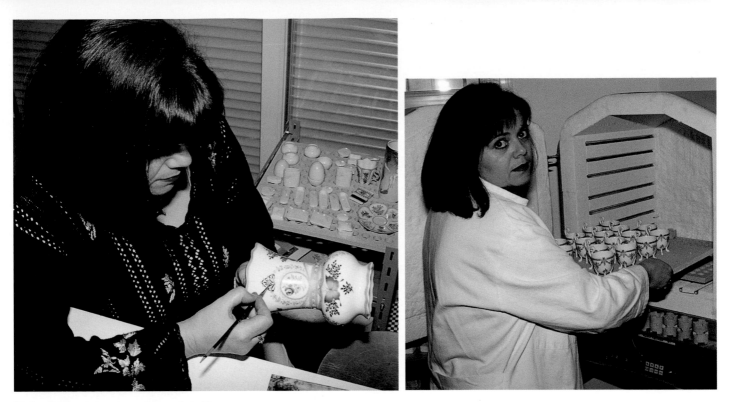

Nizète German in her decorating studio in Limoges.

Purses, 2.7" high, *Le Papillion*, *Alice* and *Colibri* patterns. Each, $208

Egg and Round Perfume, egg, 2.75" high and round perfume, 2.25" in diameter, *Le Papillion* pattern. Each, $208

Tall Box, 2.5" high, *Colibri* pattern.
$208

Heart and Purse, heart, 2" x 2" and purse, 1.6" high, *Lili* pattern. Each, $142

Egg, 2.5" high x 3.25", *Alice* pattern. $300

Footed Chests, 2" high x 2.25" x 1.75", *Marie* and *Alice* patterns. $202 and $224 respectively

Ring, Perfume and Footed Scallop Boxes, ring, 2.6" in diameter; perfume, 1.9" high; and footed scallop, 1.6" high x 3.1" x 1.9", *Alice* pattern. $186, $220, $240 respectively

Other boxes from S&D Limoges

Victor Hugo *Les Misérables*, 2.25" high, Vieille decorating mark 1, painted quill pen inside. $164

Renoir's Cats, 2.25" wide, S&D decorating mark 1, artist Florica Dragan, limited edition, painted rose inside. $202

Degas Ballerina, 3" high, porcelain ballet slippers inside. $214

Above & right: Imperial Court Monkeys, from left to right, 2.25" high, S&D decorating mark 1, limited edition of 200, and 2.75" high, unmarked S&D Limoges box, limited edition of 500. These are copies of the monkey of the Persian imperial court. The gold nut is the symbol of the monkey's status as a court amusement. Note the fine hand painting of the monkey's fur and jacket. These are two of the very best designed and decorated Limoges subject boxes. Respectively, $378 and $370

151

Egyptian Mummy, 2.5" long, $372

Talleyrand Matchbox, 3.75" high, S&D decorating mark 1, artist Florica Dragan and created from an 18th century design, available in silver or gold. $192

French Picnic Basket, 2.75" high, Vieille decorating mark 1, painted bread and wine inside. $288

California Hacienda, 2.75" high, Vieille decorating mark 1, three perfume bottles inside. $188

Swanee Paddle Boat, 2.5" high, painted riverbank with trees inside. $152

Raggedy Ann & Andy, 2.25" high, S&D decorating mark 1, artist Florica Dragan, painted *We Are Artist* outside and painted *Hi* and *MD* (Molly Dolly) inside. $220

Mademoiselle Fleurs, 2.75" high, S&D decorating mark 1, artist Florica Dragan. $160

"Victoria's Secret," 1.75" high, artist Florica Dragan, lingerie box with porcelain bra and panties inside. $174

Irish Fairy, 2.5" high, artist Florica Dragan, painted two gold hearts inside. $220

Romanian Easter Egg, 3.5" high, piece of satin material inside. $250

Mary Poppins Umbrella, 2.5" high, S&D decorating mark 1, artist Florica Dragan, blank inside. $150

Gold Harp, 3.75" high, painted gold leaf inside. $150

Butler Frog, 3.75" high, Vieille decorating mark 1, painted champagne glass inside. $224

Titanic Going Down, 1.5" high, painted patch of water and porcelain lifeboat with people inside. $138

Titanic Hitting Iceberg, 1.5" high, painted ship heading toward iceberg inside. $138

Pocket Knife, 3" high, painted mallard duck inside. $176

Basket with Champagne and Flowers, 3" high, available in three designs. $230

Pink Bunny, 2.75" high, artist Florica Dragan, painted pink rose inside. $178

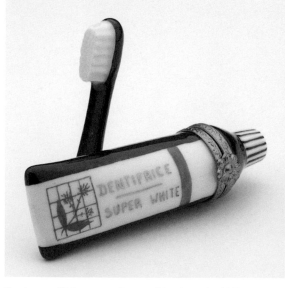

Toothpaste, 3" long, porcelain toothbrush inside. $148

154

French Champagne Frog, 2.5" high. $220

Two Herend Birds, 4" high. $260

Barn Owls, 2" high, artist Florica Dragan, painted gold feather inside. $188

Fanciful Frogs, 2" high, artist Florica Dragan, two painted gold hearts and brooch lily pad with frog inside. $194

Herend Elephant, 2.5" high, available in green or blue. $158

Rising Mallard, 2.5" high, Vieille decorating mark 1, painted cattails inside. $160

Peace Dove, S&D decorating mark 1, artist Florica Dragan, painted two gold hearts inside. $134

Courting Bunnies, 2.25" high, Vieille decorating mark 1, painted heart with arrow inside. $188

"Hear No Evil," "See No Evil," and "Speak No Evil" Monkeys, all 2.5" high, S&D decorating mark 1, artist Florica Dragan, pieces go together to form an accordion. Left to right, $210, $170, $210

Paddy the Frog, 1.75" high, Vieille decorating mark 1, painted fish on a line inside. $188

Paraguayan Parrot, 2.5" high, painted feather inside. $168

Easter Bunnies, 3.5" high. Each, $198

156

Seesawing Bears, 2.5" high, Vieille decorating mark 1, painted flowers inside, $214; Seesawing Pig and Snail, 2.5" high, Vieille decorating mark 1, painted pig and snail with fence and grass inside, $214; and Seesawing Rabbits, 2.5" high, Vieille decorating mark 1, $160

Western Boot Box, 4" high. $354

Paris Pram, 3.25" high, S&D decorating mark 1, artist Florica Dragan, porcelain baby inside. $246

Millennium Father Time, 3.75" high, Vieille decorating mark 1, porcelain sundial inside. $240

Baby's First Shoe, 2" long. $160

Heart Shaped Perfume, 2" high, Vieille decorating mark 1, painted roses and three perfume bottles inside. $188

Antique Washstand, 3" high, removable wash pitcher and wash pot. $260

Bedside Brush Set, 2.75" long, Vieille decorating mark 1, porcelain mirror and brush set inside. $188

Y2K Bug, 1.5" long, Vieille decorating mark 1, porcelain computer chip inside. $160

Schooner, 2.75" high, painted ship's helm inside. $164 .

Victorian Wash Bowl and Pitcher, 3.5" high, Vieille decorating mark 1. $198

Bedtime, 3" high, painted *warm and cozy* and porcelain bed warmer inside. $278

Doll on Cushion, 3" high, S&D decorating mark 1, artist Florica Dragan, porcelain mirror and brush set and painted rose with two buds inside. $128

Side Table, 2" high, Vieille decorating mark 1, painted gold leaf and bud and raised silver bowl with painted fruit inside. $220

Freddy Bear, 3.5" high, S&D decorating mark 1, artist Florica Dragan. $268

Cobalt Trumpet Case, 3" high, Vieille decorating mark 1, painted musical note and gold trumpet inside. $188

Standing Elf, 3.25" high, painted holly leaves inside. $162

Champ Fleur Purse, S&D decorating mark 1, artist Florica Dragan, painted rose and porcelain mirror and brush set inside. $144

Blue Hat, 2.25" high. $198

Blue Shoe, 5.5" high, artist Fiona Saunders. $250

Christmas Tree, 2.5" high, S&D decorating mark 1, artist Florica Dragan, two hearts painted inside. $140

First Love Swing, 4.5" high, artist Florica Dragan, painted *Kiss* [heart] *me* inside $270

Rabbit, 2.75" high, artist Florica Dragan. $178

Boulevard Kiosk, 3" high, Vieille decorating mark 1, $212; Pavilion Kiosk, 3" high, Vieille decorating mark 1, blank inside, $160; Metro, 2.9" high, Vieille decorating mark 1, painted raised ticket inside, $236, Eiffel Tower, 1.5" high, Vieille decorating mark 1, $102

Old World Santa, 4" high, Vieille decorating mark 1, present wrapped with a red bow inside. $288

Frog Riding Snail, 2.6" high, Parry Vieille decorating mark 1, porcelain leaf inside. $212

Asian Elephant, 2.5" high, unmarked S&D Limoges box, limited edition of 500, blue and gold painted starburst inside. This is the best decorated elephant Limoges box that we have seen. $235

Millennium Magnum/Champagne, 3.5" high, unmarked S&D Limoges, artist Florica Dragan, painted *2000/A year to remember* in gold and champagne bubbles inside. The decoration is exquisite. $225

Chamart

Chamart Display Sign

All pieces are marked Chamart.

Emperor and Empress, 3" high, introduced in 1999. Each, $200

Butterfly, 0.75" high, introduced in 1999. $230

Peacock, 2" high, introduced in 1999. $172.50

Parrot on Brass Stand, 3.75" high, introduced in 1999. $238

Golden Retriever, 4" high, introduced in 1989. $155

Carrot with Bunny, 1.24" high, introduced in 1995. $162.50

Bull and Bear, 2" high, introduced in 1999. $232.50

Cow Chef, 3.75" high, introduced in 1998. $192.50

Kangaroo with Baby, 2.75" high, introduced in 1997. $175

Elephant, 3" high, introduced in 1999. $187.50

Black and White Rooster, 4" high, introduced in 1991. $177.50

White Tiger, 4" high, introduced in 1997. $210

Rabbit with Holly, 3.75" high, introduced in 1998. $167.50

Mr. & Mrs. Frog, 4" high, introduced in 1995. Mrs. Frog, $255 and Mr. Frog, $265

Sitting Pig, 2.75" high, introduced in 1991. $235

Bull Dog Prisoner of Love, 4.25" high, introduced in 1995. $250

Millennium Valentine's Day, 2.5" high, introduced in 2000. $232.50

Millennium Mother's Day, 2.25" high, introduced in 2000. $220

Champagne Bucket, 3.5" high, introduced in 1999. $197.50

Millennium Easter Egg, 5" high, introduced in 2000. $495

Travel Journal, 1.25" high, introduced in 1998. $182.50

Gondola, 2" high, introduced in 1998. $162.50

Ballet Slippers, 2" high, introduced in 1993. $185

Lipstick, 3.5" high, introduced in 1997. $162.50

Ironing Board, 2.5" high, introduced in 1998. $187.50

Eiffel Tower, 3.25" high, introduced in 1999. $175

Cosmetic Case, 1.25" high, introduced in 1999. $230

Oval Shoe Box, 2" high, introduced in 1999, porcelain shoe inside. $182.50

Violin, 0.5" high, introduced in 1997. $177.50

Piano with Violin, 2.25" high, introduced in 1999. $247.50

Umbrella, 1" high, introduced in 1999. $135

Birthday Cake, 1.5" high, introduced in 1994. $182.50

Doctor's Bag, 1.25" high, introduced in 1997. $167.50

Menorah, 3.25" high, introduced in 1997. $162.50

Pomegranate Vase, 3" high, introduced in 1998. $172.50

Apples on Plate, 1.5" high, introduced in 1997. $185

Nativity, 2.75" high, introduced in 1998. $297.50

Bottle of Red Wine, 3" high, introduced in 1997. $132.50

Flower Box, 1.25" high, limited edition, introduced in 1999. $262.50

Stack of Plates with Cheese, 2" high, introduced in 1997, $247.50; Tray with Pasta and Wine, 2.5" high, introduced in 1997, $257.50; and Case of Wine, 1" high, introduced in 1996, $177.50

Water Lily, 1.25" high, introduced in 1999. $175

Tobacco Leaf Perfume Egg, 2.25" high, introduced in 1996. $237.50

Flower Basket, 2" high, limited edition, introduced in 1998. $295

Footed Lily of the Valley Egg, 2.5" high, introduced in 1998. $220

Pansy Heart, 2" high, introduced in 1998, painted *I Love You* inside. $315

Garden Arbor, 3" high, introduced in 1999. $192.50

Daisy, 1" high, introduced in 1991. $127.50

Two Peas in a Pod, 1" high, introduced in 1995. $175

Round Box Egaltine/Fruits, 1.5" high, introduced in 1999. $262.50

Easter Egg Basket, 3" high, introduced in 1997. $157.50

To Mother with Love Envelope, 1.25" high, introduced in 1999, separate porcelain piece inside. $210

Oval with Tulips in Relief, 1" high, introduced in 1989. $157.50

Ring Heart Box, 1" high, introduced in 1998. $187.50

170

Cookbook, 1" high, introduced in 1995. $182.50

Frying Pan with Eggs, 0.5" high, introduced in 1996. $157.50

Rochard

Rochard Display Sign

Fruit and Vegetable Folks, left to right, Green Pepper Man, 2.6" high; Pineapple Man, 2.9" high; Corn Man, 2.5" high; Banana Man, 2.9" high; Peapod Man, 3.1" high; and Radish Man, 2.6" high. All boxes have Rochard decorating mark 3 and are blank inside. Each, $170

Buddah, 3" x 2.5", Rochard decorating mark 3, painted butterfly inside. This box is photographed on the front cover of the Rochard book on Limoges boxes (see Bibliography). $260

Harley Davidson Motorcycle, 2.25" high, Rochard decorating mark 1, painted helmet inside. $270

Violin and Maplewood Case, 3" x 1.25", Rochard decorating mark 4, blank inside. $220

Pinball Machine, 3.1" high, Rochard decorating mark 3, painted *Gagné!* inside. $230

Baby Carriage with Parasol, 3.5" high, Rochard decorating mark 2, painted pacifier inside. $160

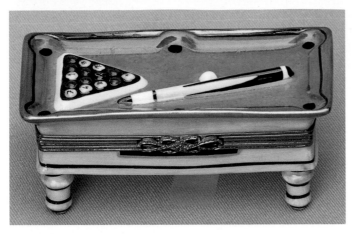

Billiard Table, 1.1" high, Rochard decorating mark 2, painted wisp inside. $280

Sunflower, 3.25" high, Rochard decorating mark 3, blank inside. $180

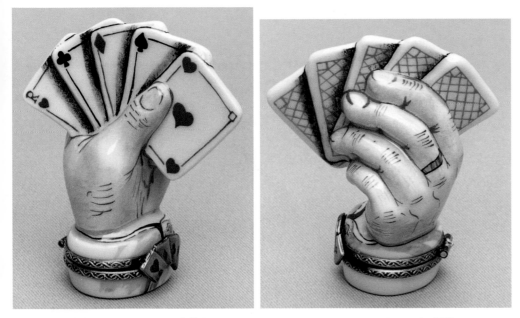

Sleight of Hand (front and back), 2.9" high, Rochard decorating mark 4, painted dice inside. $180

Heart Jewel Box, 2.6" high, Rochard decorating mark 3, painted red heart on gold chain inside. $140

Foxglove, 3.25" high, Rochard decorating mark 3, blank inside. $170

Watering Can, 2.1" high, Rochard decorating mark 3, painted wisp inside. $150

Cala Lily, 3.25" high, Rochard decorating mark 3, blank inside. $170

Rabbit in Basket with Easter Eggs, 2.75" high, Rochard decorating mark 3, painted blue ribbon inside. $190

Blue Amaryllis, 3.25" high, Rochard decorating mark 3, blank inside. $170

Pink Amaryllis, 3.25" high, Rochard decorating mark 3, blank inside. $170

Chicken in Basket with Easter Eggs, 2.75" high, Rochard decorating mark 3, painted blue ribbon inside. $190

Cameramen, 3.25" high, Rochard decorating mark 2, painted strip of film inside. $240

Chick in Gold Egg, 1" high, Rochard decorating mark 4, porcelain chick inside. $150

Easel with Paints, 3.4" high, Rochard decorating mark 3, two porcelain tubes of paint inside. $270

Ballet Slippers, 1.75" x 1.75", Rochard decorating mark 3, painted music notes inside. $220

Dress Forms, 2.9" high, Rochard decorating mark 2, blank inside. Each, $160.

Rochard Shopping Bag, 3" high, Rochard decorating mark 3, painted gift box inside. $140

Tea Caddy, 2.25" high, Rochard decorating mark 4, painted flower inside. $200

Floral Telephone, 2.1" high, Rochard decorating mark 3, painted flowers inside. $190

Fruit Compote, 1.75" high, Rochard decorating mark 3, blank inside. $160

Typewriter, 1.5" high, Rochard decorating mark 3, blank inside. $120

Washing Machine, 1.9" high, Rochard decorating mark 3, blank inside. $170

Serving Cart, 3.75" high, Rochard decorating mark 2. $350

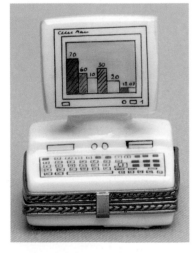

Computer, 1.75" high, Rochard decorating mark 3, painted computer mouse inside. $180

Watermelon, 1.75" high, Rochard decorating mark 3, painted flower inside. $150

Hippo in Bathtub, 2" high, Rochard decorating mark 3, blank inside. $210

Frog in Evening Gear, 1.75" high, Rochard decorating mark 4, painted money inside. $190

Panda, 1.9" high, Richard decorating mark 4, painted bamboo inside. $220

Lion in Evening Gear, 2" high, Rochard decorating mark 4, painted money inside. $170

Owl in Evening Gear, 2.6" high, Rochard decorating mark 4, painted money inside. $180

Polar Bear and Cub, 2.6" high, Rochard decorating mark 3, painted fish inside. $220

Koala Bears, 2.9" high, Rochard decorating mark 3, painted leaves inside. $230

Mini Kitten, 1.7" high, Rochard decorating mark 4, painted ball of yarn inside. $130

Leopard, 1.9" high, Rochard decorating mark 2, painted wisp inside. $190

Kitten in a Basket, 3" high, Rochard decorating mark 3, painted ball of yarn inside. $190

Dog with Dog House, 2.5" high, Rochard decorating mark 3, painted gold bone inside. $220

Two Mice on a See-saw, 3" high, Rochard decorating mark 2, painted sailor hat and anchor inside. $390

Swan, 2" high, Rochard decorating mark 4, painted nest with eggs inside. $190

Right: Pink Crested Cockatoo, 3.4" high, Rochard decorating mark 4, painted peanut inside. $250

Birdcage with Two Birds, 4.25" high, Rochard decorating mark 4, painted gold bird inside. $350

Toucan, 3" high, Rochard decorating mark 4, painted berries and leaves inside. $250

Butterfly, 2" high, Rochard decorating mark 4, painted flowers inside. $190

Tropical Fish, 3.9" high, Rochard decorating mark 4, painted sea plants. Each, $250

Turtle, 1.75" high, Rochard decorating mark 4, painted plants on bottom. $180

Santa by Fireplace, 2.75" high, Rochard decorating mark 3, painted scarf inside. $390

Lighthouse, 3.25" high, Rochard decorating mark 3, painted trees inside. $230

Crystal Turtle, 2" high, Rochard decorating mark
5. $250

Snow Surfers, 2.6" high, Rochard decorating mark 2, painted wisp inside.
$210

Crystal Cat and Kitten, 2.75" high, Rochard decorating mark
5. $260

Golf Cart, 2.25" high, Rochard decorating mark 2, painted golf
clubs inside and separate porcelain golf bag. $270

Crystal Mermaid, 2.4" high, Rochard decorating mark 5.
$260

Artoria

The Millennium Collection

Artoria Display Sign

The Millennium Collection

Y2K Bug, 3" high, Artoria decorating mark 5, porcelain baby Y2K bug inside. $280

Millennium Lion and Lamb, 2.5" high, Artoria decorating mark 2, *The New Millennium/An Era of Peace* in black script inside. $178

Goose with the Golden Egg, 3.25" high, Artoria decorating mark 5, edition of 1/1,000, *A Prosperous New Millennium* in black script and a porcelain gold egg inside. $170

Millennium Champagne Glasses, 2.75" high, Artoria decorating mark 5, *Happy New Millennium* in gold script inside. $224

Millennium Globe, 2.75" high, Artoria decorating mark 2, *For Celebration of the New Millennium* on outside of globe, inside blank. $250

Eiffel Tower 2000, 3.75" high, Artoria decorating mark 5, porcelain champagne bottle inside. $224

End of Millenium group

Imperial Elephant, 3" high, Artoria decorating mark 2, inside blank. $238

Camel with Aladdin's Lamp, 3.25" high, Artoria decorating mark 2, inside blank. $238

Hurdy-Gurdy Monkey, 2.5" high, Artoria decorating mark 2, inside blank. $238

Fortune Cookie, 1.5" high, Artoria decorating mark 5, *You Will Have Good Fortune* on porcelain sign inside. $130

Wall Street Bear and Wall Street Bull, each 3.5" high, Artoria decorating mark 2, porcelain gold coin inside each box. Bear, $206 and bull, $196

Angelic Animals

Angelic Black Sheep, 2.75" high, Artoria decorating mark 5, edition of 3/1,000, painted sheep breaking through a fence inside. $234

Angelic Pig in Tub, 3.5" high, Artoria decorating mark 2, porcelain scrub brush inside. $210

Angelic Dog, 3.5" high, Artoria decorating mark 5, painted black paw print inside. $204

Angelic Puppy, 2" high, Artoria decorating mark 5, edition of 1/1,000, painted chewed up shoe inside. $228

Angelic Pig, 3.25" high, Artoria decorating mark 5, painted banana split inside. $250

Angelic Cat, 3" high, Artoria decorating mark 5, painted cat's face inside. $196

Mickey Sorcerer/Fantasia 2000/©Disney, 2.25" high, Artoria decorating mark 2, separate porcelain bucket brigade piece and painted bucket brigade inside. $278

Two Mushrooms/Fantasia 60th Anniversary/©Disney, 2.25" high and 3.25" high respectively, Artoria decorating mark 2, blank inside. Small mushroom (Hop Low), $144 and large mushroom, $176.

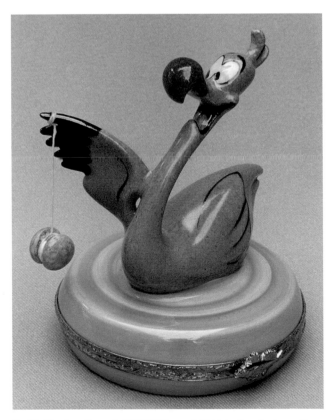

Punkin Flamingo/Fantasia 2000/©Disney, 3.5" high, Artoria decorating mark 2, painted yo-yo inside. $236

The Zodiac Collection

Inside each box in gold script is the name of the zodiac sign, all boxes have Artoria decorating mark 2, and each box is valued at $170.

Aries (Ram), 2" high, March 21-April 19.

Taurus (Bull), 1.75" high, April 20-May 20.

Gemini (Twins), 2" high, May 21-June 21.

Cancer (Crab), 1.4" high, June 22-July 22.

Leo (Lion), 1.75" high, July 23-August 22.

Virgo (Virgin), 2" high, August 23-September 22.

Libra (Balance), 2.25" high, September 23-
October 23.

Scorpio (Scorpion), 1.75" high, October 24-
November 21.

Sagittarius (Archer), 2.25" high, November
22-December 21.

Capricorn (Goat), 2" high, December 22-
January 19.

Aquarius (Water Bearer), 2.1" high, January
20-February 18.

Pisces (Fish), 1.25" high, February 19-March
20.

Nativity Scene

All boxes have Artoria decorating mark 2.

Boxes from left to right are as follows: Shepherd, 3.5" high, painted sheep inside, $198; Wiseman, purple, 3.9" high, painted herbal container inside, $214; Wiseman, blue, 4.4" high, painted herbal container inside, $214; Joseph, 3.5" high, painted barn with cradle, sheep and moon inside, $192; Angel, 3.5" high, painted sun over clouds inside, $192; Baby Jesus, 1.5" high, painted child with halo inside, $192; Wiseman, green, 3.5" high, painted herbal container inside, $214; Mary, 3.25" high, painted mountain with moon and star inside, $198; Camel, 3" high, painted star over mountains with road inside, $198; Donkey, 2.5" high, painted star over mountains with road inside, $198; and Ox, 2.5" high, painted star over mountains with road inside, $198.

Two Birds in a Nest, 2.1" high, Artoria decorating mark 2, painted hatching chick inside. $224

Rooster, 4.4" high, Artoria decorating mark 2, painted flower inside. $230

Giraffe, 4.5" high, Artoria decorating mark 2, painted green leaves inside. $202

Single Monkey, 3.6" high, Artoria porcelain mark 1 and Artoria decorating mark 2, painted pineapple inside. $202

Tiger, 2.5" high, Artoria decorating mark 2, painted elephant inside. $196

All American Fast Food

Diner, 3.1" high x 1.5" x 1.9", Artoria decorating mark 2, painted hamburger and milk shake inside. $152

Hot Dog, 2.25" long, Artoria decorating mark 2, painted mustard bottle inside. $98

Hamburger and French Fries, fries, 1.9" high and hamburger, 1.6" in diameter, both Artoria decorating mark 2, both with painted bottle of ketchup inside. Each, $98

Banana Split, 2.75" high, Artoria decorating mark 2, two cherries painted inside. $118

Ice Cream Sundae, 2.75" high, Artoria decorating mark 2, blank inside. $118

Strawberry Ice Cream Cone, 2.1" high, Artoria decorating mark 2, painted strawberry inside. $96

Ice Cream Cone with Sprinkles, 2.1" high, Artoria decorating mark 2, painted vanilla beans inside. $134

Popcorn, 1.75" high, Artoria decorating mark 2, painted movie projector inside. $98

Muffin Tin with Cup Cakes, 3.1" x 1.75", Artoria decorating mark 2, painted serving knife inside. $224

Hawthorne Basket, 2.1" high, Artoria decorating mark 5, three glass bottles and sprig of hawthorn painted inside. $208

Hawthorne Purse, 1.5" high, Artoria decorating mark 2, two sprigs of hawthorn painted inside. $168

Oval Hawthorne, 1" high, Artoria decorating mark 5, painted sprig of hawthorn inside. $162

Impresario Purple Piano, 1.4" high, Artoria decorating mark 5, painted gold leaf inside. $178

Egg with Ferns, 1.6" high, Artoria decorating mark 2, painted gold leaf inside. $168

Bachelor Button Basket, 2.1" high, Artoria decorating mark 5, three glass bottles and sprig of bachelor buttons painted inside. $208

Impresario Purple Egg, 2.1" high, Artoria decorating mark 2, painted gold leaf inside. $178

Cylinder with Ferns, 2.75" high, Artoria decorating mark 2, blank inside. $162

Bachelor Button Armchair, 2.25" high, Artoria decorating mark 5, painted sprig of bachelor buttons inside. $178

Small Impresario Purple Square, 1.1" square, Artoria decorating mark 5, painted gold leaf inside. $162

Small Square with Ferns, 1.1" square, Artoria decorating mark 5, painted gold leaf inside. $162

Small Round Bachelor Button, 1.25" in diameter, Artoria decorating mark 5, painted sprig of bachelor buttons inside. $162

Medium Round Impresario Magenta, 2" in diameter, Artoria decorating mark 2, painted gold leaf inside. $178

Small Round Impresario Magenta, 1.25" in diameter, Artoria decorating mark 5, painted gold leaf inside. $162

Impresario Magenta Heart, 1.1" high, Artoria decorating mark 2, painted gold leaf inside. $168

Impresario Magenta Tent, 1.75" high, Artoria decorating mark 5, painted gold leaf inside. $168

Dubarry

The Prince's Trust Masks

The Prince's Trust was set up in 1976 to help disadvantaged young people reach their ambitions. There were 458 painted clay masks that were created by leading celebrities from art, music, theater, film, politics, sports and business. The original masks were auctioned in 1996 by Sotheby's, and Dubarry obtained the rights in 1997 to reproduce these masks in porcelain. All boxes measure 2.5" x 3.6."

Dubarry Display Sign.

194

Every mask box has this Prince's Trust inscription.

Marks on the bottom of all The Prince's Trust masks.

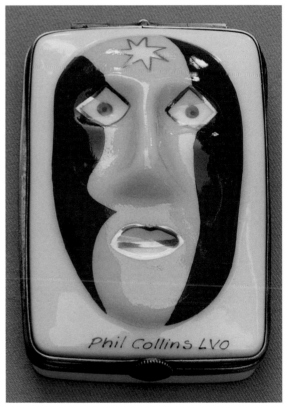

Phil Collins Mask. $178

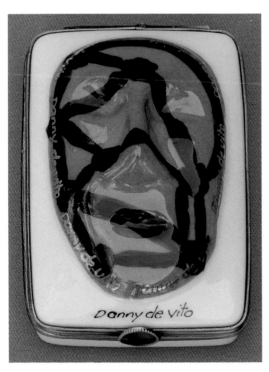

Danny de Vito Mask. $178

Placido Domingo Mask. $178

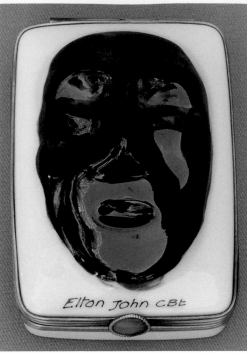

Elton John Mask. $144

Bette Midler Mask. $178

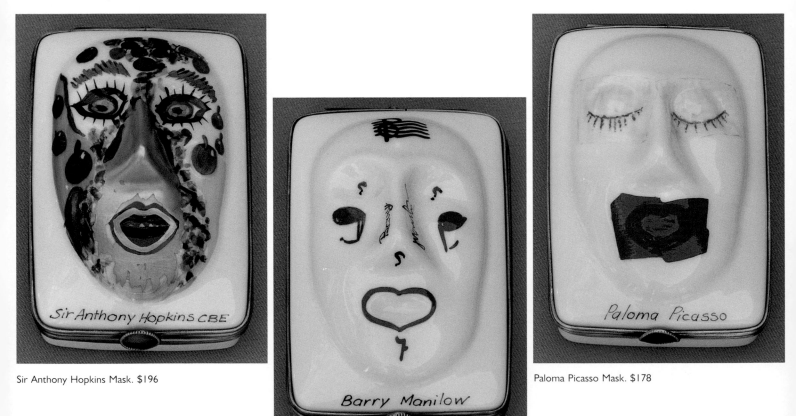

Sir Anthony Hopkins Mask. $196

Barry Manilow Mask. $178

Paloma Picasso Mask. $178

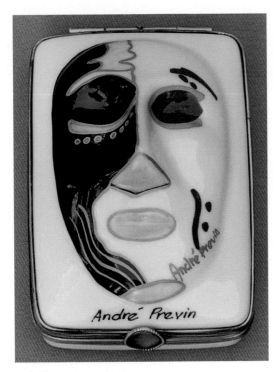

André Previn Mask. $178

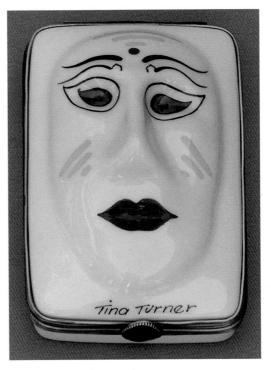

Tina Turner Mask. $178

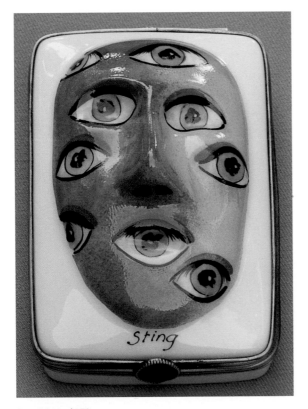

Sting Mask. $178

Alice's Journey Through Wonderland

The designs of these boxes are based upon the paintings by Angel Dominguez in the 1996 edition of the Lewis Carroll book (see Bibliography).

Alice, 2.9" high, Dubarry decorating mark 5, blank inside. $250

Mad Hatter with Tea Table, hatter, 4" high, Dubarry decorating mark 1, and tea table, 2.25" high, Dubarry decorating mark 5. Set, $326

White Rabbit, 3" high, Dubarry decorating mark 1, painted gold pocket watch inside. $220

Cheshire Cat, 2" high, Dubarry decorating mark 5, blank inside. $174

Caterpillar, 2.5" high, Dubarry decorating mark 1, blank inside. $182

Queen of Hearts, 2.25" high, Dubarry decorating mark 5, blank inside. $318

Fabergé Eggs, each 2.75" high and each with Dubarry decorating mark 2. Egg on left, limited edition, 510/1000, $274; egg in center, limited edition, 294/500, $300; and egg on right, $288. A glass perfume bottle is found inside each egg.

Green Empire Boxes, egg on left, 1.6" high, painted gold and green starburst inside, $206; upright box, center rear, 1.9" high, two glass bottles inside, $222; heart box on right, 1.25" high, painted gold and green starburst inside, $206; and round box, front center, 1.1" high, painted gold and green starburst inside, $210. All have Dubarry decorating mark 1.

Red Empire Eggs, egg on left, 2.75" high, red glass bottle inside, $232; egg on right, 1.6" high, painted red and gold starburst, $210. Both have Dubarry decorating mark 1.

Dubarry Millennium Boxes

Millennium Teddys, from left to right, Centurion Teddy 2000, 3.25" high, Dubarry decorating mark 2, painted champagne flutes inside, $220; Graduation Year 2000 Teddy, 2.5" high, Dubarry decorating mark 2, painted *Congratulations* in gold inside, $214; Millennium Birthday Teddy, 2.6" high, Dubarry decorating mark 1, blank inside, $248; and Champagne for 2000 Teddy, 3" high, Dubarry decorating mark 2, painted champagne flutes inside, $216.

USA Y2K Cube, 1.1" high, Dubarry decorating mark 1, porcelain champagne bottle inside. $232

Teddy Welcoming the Year 2000, 1.6" square, Dubarry decorating mark 1, porcelain teddy bear and porcelain sign inside. $220

Hello Sunny 2000, 1.75" in diameter, Dubarry decorating mark 1, porcelain sun and painted *Hello 2000!* inside. $184

Salt & Pepper Mill, 2" high, Dubarry decorating mark 1, blank inside. $168

Rialto Blue Shopping Bag, 2.5" high, Dubarry decorating mark 2, painted gold wisp inside. $130

Easter Egg Teddy, 1.6" high, Dubarry decorating mark 1, limited edition, 260/500, blank inside. $216

Cooking Range, 2.25" high, Dubarry decorating mark 5, blank inside. $236

Sewing Machine, 2" high, Dubarry decorating mark 1, blank inside. $214

Pot Belly Stove, 2.9" high, Dubarry decorating mark 1, blank inside. $180

Papillon Handbag, 2.25" high, Dubarry decorating mark 1, painted green leaf inside. $162

201

Airline Case, 2.75" high, Dubarry decorating mark 1. $240

Train, 2.6" x 2", Dubarry decorating mark 1. $244

Monet Bridge, 1.5" high, no decorating company mark. $230

Geisha, 2.25" high, Dubarry decorating mark 1, painted gold leaf inside. $214

Shooting the Rapids, 1.4" high, French & Pacific Trading decorating mark 1, painted man in canoe inside. $300

Camping Holiday, 2.75" x 1.6", no company mark, painted rope and compass inside. $264

Eiffel Tower, 3.9" high, no company mark, painted red heart with Paris inside heart. $150

Leaning Tower of Pisa, 3.25" high, no company mark, painted blue wisp inside. $240

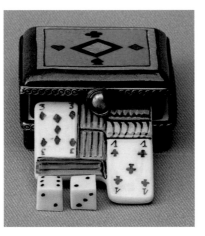

Compendium of Games, 1.25" square, Dubarry decorating mark 1, porcelain cards, playing chips, and dice. $232

New York Harbor, 2.25" high, no company mark, painted blue wisp inside. $140

Chair, 2.25" high, Dubarry decorating mark 5, painted gold wisp inside. $140

Christmas Teddys, from left to right, Teddy on Skis, 2.5" high, painted present inside, $148; Teddy with Christmas Tree, 3" high, painted scarf inside, $224; and Christmas Time, 2.4" high, painted present inside, $236. All have Dubarry decorating mark 5.

Christmas Gift, 1.9" high, no company mark, blank inside. $170

Country House, 2.4" high, French & Pacific Trading decorating mark 1, painted blue flowers and green leaves inside. $316

Santa with Children, 2.4" high, blank inside. $316

The Last Supper, 2.4" high x 4.4" x 1.9", painted gold wisp inside. $520

Carousel, 3.5" high, French & Pacific Trading decorating mark 1, painted gold wisp inside. $370

Child's Cupboard, 1.3" high. $312

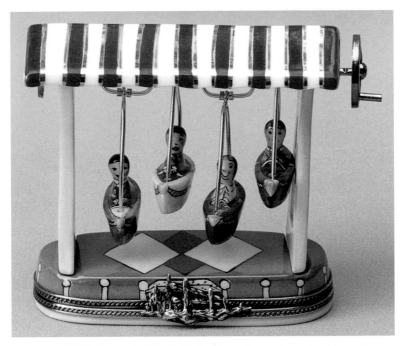

Boat Swing, 3.6" high, French & Pacific Trading decorating mark 1, painted boy with balloons inside. $480

Limoges Collectors Society

Limoges Collectors
Society Display Sign.

Three Clowns, all 3.25" high, Limoges
Collectors decorating mark. From left to
right: $115, $129, and $115

Miss Piggy and Opera Piggy, 4" and 4.25" high, Limoges
Collectors decorating mark. Miss Piggy, $125 and Opera
Piggy, $100.

Mouse, 3.5" high, Limoges Collectors decorating mark. $155

Cheese Dome, 2" high, Limoges Collectors decorating mark. $98

Walrus, 4" high, Limoges Collectors decorating mark. $99

Millennium Eiffel Tower, 3.75" high, Ribierre mark 1, current, and in script on bottom, *Limoges Collectors Society*. Also, *Millennium/ 01.01.00/Thomas & Keith* in gold and *Bonne Année 2000*, and painted champagne cork inside. $225

Garden Bench Swing, 3.5" high, Limoges Collectors decorating mark. $149

Other Boxes

Fish Grouping, each 2.5" high, Parry Vieille decorating mark 1. These fish, which are available in different colors and patterns, are reminiscent of the glass fish made by Lalique, which come in 24 different colors. These brightly colored fish are especially attractive when grouped together in a school. Each, $195

Cobalt Oval Box, 1.5" high x 3.4" in diameter, Tharaud decorating mark 1.1, 1920-1945, and overglaze decorating mark in red, *DEPIERREFICHE*. We are not familiar with this decorating mark, but this piece combines hand painted gold trim with gold transfers. It is unusual to find relatively early Tharaud porcelain blanks with the marks of other decorators. $60-$75

Unhinged Oval Floral Box, 1.9" high x 2.5" x 1.75", T. Haviland decorating mark t in blue, 1967—. There are colorful flowers on the lid of this box. $25-$40

Unhinged Eagle Box, 1.25" high x 2.5" x 1.9", T. Haviland decorating mark t in blue, 1967—. The colors and pattern on this box are the same as those on the Lincoln dinnerware. $25-$40

Unhinged Oval Eagle Box, 1.9" high x 2.5" x 1.75", T. Haviland decorating mark t in blue, 1967—. $25-$40

Company Histories and Marks

We have included over 500 marks of Limoges porcelain manufacturers, decorators, exporters, and importers. This section has been revised and expanded to include new information between our first book and the present one. Since there is not presently a lot of data even about some of the larger companies, we will continue to revise the dating of some marks as new information becomes available. Furthermore, there will always be a large number of marks that will be difficult or impossible to identify and/or date. Only companies that exported their wares were required to file registrations. Since registration was costly, many of the smaller companies never registered, so there are no public records of their businesses.

We used many sources to date the marks in this book. We have relied upon our personal knowledge of Limoges porcelain, and we have drawn on numerous sources, including d'Albis and Romanet, Tardy, Mannoni, *Chefs-d'Oeuvre de la Porcelaine de Limoges*, Cushion, Cameron, Henderson, *Celebrating 150 Years of Haviland China*, and Gaston (see Bibliography) and discussions with people familiar with some of the companies.

We have also provided diagrams, which outline the histories of many of the Limoges porcelain companies. The dating of specific events in the histories of these companies oftentimes provides clues on the use and dates of specific marks.

Some of the numbers that we have assigned to marks within the same company are out of numerical sequence and others are not whole numbers, such as *0.5* or *1.1*, for example. This was intentional so that the mark numbers in this book would be the same as the mark numbers in our previous book. This facilitates referencing the company marks in many different forums.

Finally, we have included photographs of several different "fake" Limoges marks. Most of the pieces with these marks originate in Asia. Unscrupulous sellers advertise them as Limoges, with the clear implication that they are from Limoges, France. The Internet auction sites are flooded with these pieces. The two characteristics these marks have in common are the word *Limoges* and the absence of the word *France*. Since the McKinley Tariff bill in 1891, nearly all porcelain imported into the U.S. was stamped with the name of the country of origin. There are rare exceptions, for example "connoisseur" pieces made by C. Tharaud, but certainly all contemporary pieces imported from Limoges have as part of their mark the word, *France*.

Company Histories

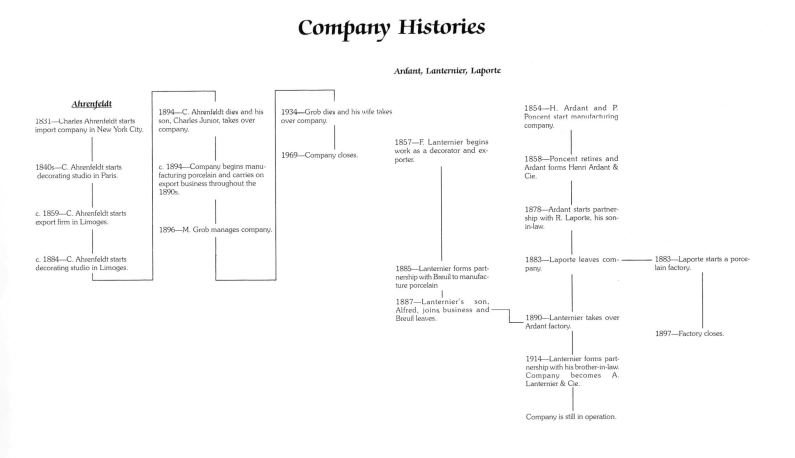

Ardant, Lanternier, Laporte

Ahrenfeldt

1831—Charles Ahrenfeldt starts import company in New York City.

1840s—C. Ahrenfeldt starts decorating studio in Paris.

c. 1859—C. Ahrenfeldt starts export firm in Limoges.

c. 1884—C. Ahrenfeldt starts decorating studio in Limoges.

1894—C. Ahrenfeldt dies and his son, Charles Junior, takes over company.

c. 1894—Company begins manufacturing porcelain and carries on export business throughout the 1890s.

1896—M. Grob manages company.

1934—Grob dies and his wife takes over company.

1969—Company closes.

1857—F. Lanternier begins work as a decorator and exporter.

1885—Lanternier forms partnership with Breuil to manufacture porcelain.

1887—Lanternier's son, Alfred, joins business and Breuil leaves.

1914—Lanternier forms partnership with his brother-in-law. Company becomes A. Lanternier & Cie.

Company is still in operation.

1854—H. Ardant and P. Poncent start manufacturing company.

1858—Poncent retires and Ardant forms Henri Ardant & Cie.

1878—Ardant starts partnership with R. Laporte, his son-in-law.

1883—Laporte leaves company.

1890—Lanternier takes over Ardant factory.

1883—Laporte starts a porcelain factory.

1897—Factory closes.

Comte d'Artois, Ancienne Manufacture Royale, Alluaud, C.F. Haviland, GDM, GDA

1773—Comte d'Artois becomes patron of A. Massié, Grellet and Fournerat factory.

1784—Factory purchased by King Louis XVI and becomes Manufacture Royale, a subsidiary of Sèvres. Younger Grellet brother becomes director.

1788—François Alluaud becomes director.

1793—Factory becomes national company and named Ancienne Manufacture Royale.

1794—Company disrupted by French Revolution.

1796—Three former employees—Joly, Joubert, Cacate—purchase factory, and Alluaud leases Joly's share.

1817—Pierre Tharaud takes over company. Company taken over by others in successive years.

1929-1986—Société Porcelainière uses name of Ancienne Manufacture Royale.

1986—Bernardaud & Cie and M. Denis Verspieren (Société B.V. Porcelaine) buys company.

Company still in operation.

1798/1799—Alluaud starts own factory and dies the next year. His son, F. Alluaud, takes over.

1814—Alluaud and his brother, Jean Baptiste Clément, create new company, Alluaud Frères.

1823—Clément leaves company.

1872—F. Bracquemond becomes director of decorating studio.

1852—C.F. Haviland works for uncle, D. Haviland

1859—Haviland starts small decorating studio with uncle, Richard Haviland. Studio decorates Alluaud pieces for export to New York.

1865—Haviland begins partnership with father, Robert B. Haviland, and brother, F. Haviland, to rent factory for manufacturing porcelain.

Before 1870—Haviland starts decorating studio.

1870—Haviland starts manufacturing company with O. Gager and forms Charles Field Haviland & Cie.

1876—Haviland takes over Alluaud factory in Casseaux.

1881—E. Gérard, J.B. Dufraisseix, and Morel form GDM and take over Haviland company. Haviland retires.

1890—Morel leaves GDM. Firm called GD.

1895—S. Bing, expert in Japanese arts, starts Art Nouveau style and contracts with GD.

1900—GD's American agent, E. Abbot, joins firm. Firm called GDA.

1929—With worldwide financial crisis of 1929, GDA purchases C.F. Haviland mark.

1941—R. Haviland, grandson of C.F. Haviland, purchases C.F. Haviland mark.

1950—GDA is managed by Raymond Clappier.

Company is still in operation.

Baignol, Berger, Michelaud, Jammet & Seignolles

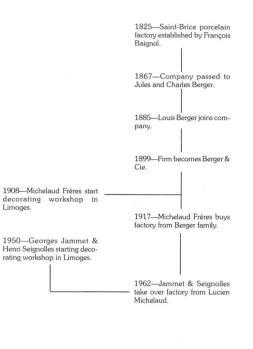

1825—Saint-Brice porcelain factory established by François Baignol.

1867—Company passed to Jules and Charles Berger.

1885—Louis Berger joins company.

1899—Firm becomes Berger & Cie.

1908—Michelaud Frères start decorating workshop in Limoges.

1917—Michelaud Frères buys factory from Berger family.

1950—Georges Jammet & Henri Seignolles starting decorating workshop in Limoges.

1962—Jammet & Seignolles take over factory from Lucien Michelaud.

Délinières, Bernardaud, Vignaud, Serpaut

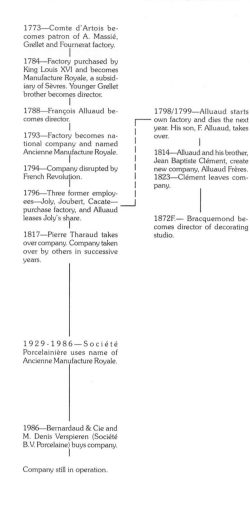

1860s—R. Délinières and P. Guéry start company.

1879—Délinières heads up company.

1900—L. Bernardaud takes over company, which is named L. Bernardaud & Cie.

1911—A. Vignaud starts company.

1920—C. Serpaut leaves Bernardaud and starts own company.

1930—Serpaut's son takes over company.

Late 1950s—Company closes.

1970—Bernardaud buys Vignaud.

1986—Bernardaud buys half of Ancienne Manufacture Royale.

Company is still in operation.

Gibus, Redon, Barny & Rigoni, Porcelaine Limousine, Chastagner

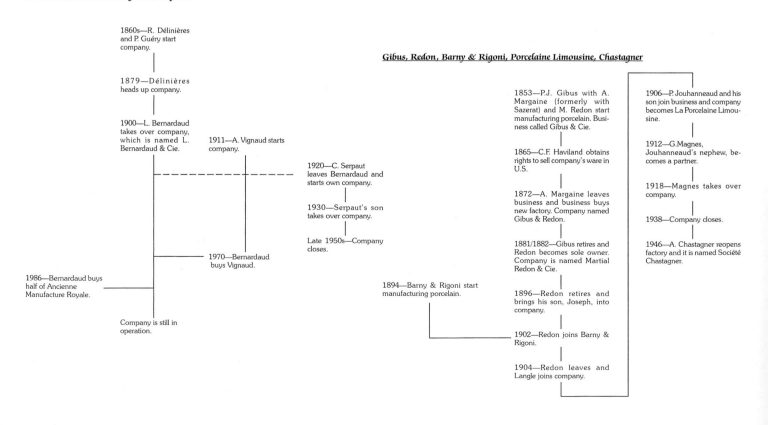

1853—P.J. Gibus with A. Margaine (formerly with Sazerat) and M. Redon start manufacturing porcelain. Business called Gibus & Cie.

1865—C.F. Haviland obtains rights to sell company's ware in U.S.

1872—A. Margaine leaves business and business buys new factory. Company named Gibus & Redon.

1881/1882—Gibus retires and Redon becomes sole owner. Company is named Martial Redon & Cie.

1894—Barny & Rigoni start manufacturing porcelain.

1896—Redon retires and brings his son, Joseph, into company.

1902—Redon joins Barny & Rigoni.

1904—Redon leaves and Langle joins company.

1906—P. Jouhanneaud and his son join business and company becomes La Porcelaine Limousine.

1912—G. Magnes, Jouhanneaud's nephew, becomes a partner.

1918—Magnes takes over company.

1938—Company closes.

1946—A. Chastagner reopens factory and it is named Société Chastagner.

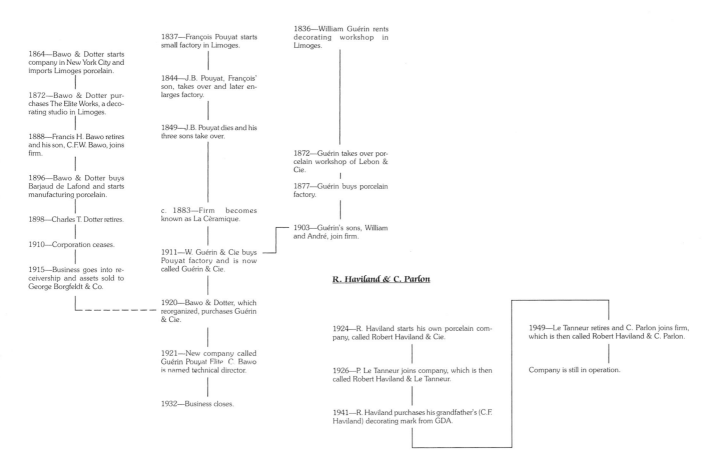

1864—Bawo & Dotter starts company in New York City and imports Limoges porcelain.

1872—Bawo & Dotter purchases The Elite Works, a decorating studio in Limoges.

1888—Francis H. Bawo retires and his son, C.F.W. Bawo, joins firm.

1896—Bawo & Dotter buys Barjaud de Lafond and starts manufacturing porcelain.

1898—Charles T. Dotter retires.

1910—Corporation ceases.

1915—Business goes into receivership and assets sold to George Borgfeldt & Co.

1837—François Pouyat starts small factory in Limoges.

1844—J.B. Pouyat, François' son, takes over and later enlarges factory.

1849—J.B. Pouyat dies and his three sons take over.

c. 1883—Firm becomes known as La Cèramique.

1911—W. Guérin & Cie buys Pouyat factory and is now called Guérin & Cie.

1920—Bawo & Dotter, which reorganized, purchases Guérin & Cie.

1921—New company called Guérin Pouyat Elite C. Bawo is named technical director.

1932—Business closes.

1836—William Guérin rents decorating workshop in Limoges.

1872—Guérin takes over porcelain workshop of Lebon & Cie.

1877—Guérin buys porcelain factory.

1903—Guérin's sons, William and André, join firm.

R. Haviland & C. Parlon

1924—R. Haviland starts his own porcelain company, called Robert Haviland & Cie.

1926—P. Le Tanneur joins company, which is then called Robert Haviland & Le Tanneur.

1941—R. Haviland purchases his grandfather's (C.F. Haviland) decorating mark from GDA.

1949—Le Tanneur retires and C. Parlon joins firm, which is then called Robert Haviland & C. Parlon.

Company is still in operation.

Haviland Family Tree

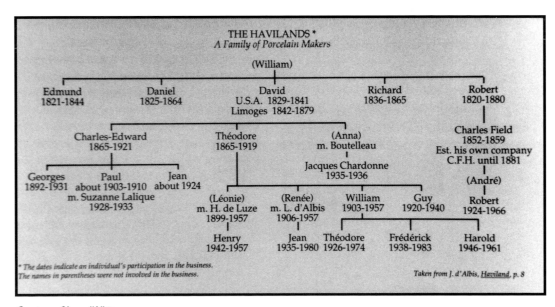

THE HAVILANDS *
A Family of Porcelain Makers

(William)

| Edmund 1821-1844 | Daniel 1825-1864 | David U.S.A. 1829-1841 Limoges 1842-1879 | Richard 1836-1865 | Robert 1820-1880 |

Charles-Edward 1865-1921 — Théodore 1865-1919 — (Anna) m. Boutelleau

Jacques Chardonne 1935-1936

Charles Field 1852-1859 Est. his own company C.F.H. until 1881

(André)

Georges 1892-1931 — Paul about 1903-1910 m. Suzanne Lalique 1928-1933 — Jean about 1924

(Léonie) m. H. de Luze 1899-1957 — (Renée) m. L. d'Albis 1906-1957 — William 1903-1957 — Guy 1920-1940

Robert 1924-1966

Henry 1942-1957 — Jean 1935-1980 — Théodore 1926-1974 — Frédérick 1938-1983 — Harold 1946-1961

*The dates indicate an individual's participation in the business. The names in parentheses were not involved in the business.

Taken from J. d'Albis, *Haviland*, p. 8

Courtesy of Jean d'Albis

Latrille, Mavaleix & Granger, Balleroy

1899—Latrille Frères start factory.

Early 1900s—P.M. Mavaleix, Mandavy and H. Balleroy start firm.

1908—J. Granger joins business.

1908—Mavaleix starts his own business.

1908—H. Balleroy and brother, Antoine, for new business, Balleroy Frères.

1913—J. Granger leaves and company closes.

1914—Mavaleix closes business during World War I.

1920—Granger joins Mavaleix to reopen business.

1922—Granger heads up Mavaleix factory.

c. 1937—Business closes.

1938—Business closes.

Paroutaud, Maigner, Union Porcelainière, Limoges Porcelaine, Porcelaine Lafarge

1895—Mme Vue Paroutaud and her two sons, Pierre and Paul, start manufacturing company.

1928—Company becomes Union Porcelainière with Demarty & H. Lafarge as principals.

1902—Paroutaud Frères take over company.

1941—Lafarge and N. Nardon create Limoges Porcelaine.

1916—Paroutaud Frères leave and company becomes Maigner & Cie. It is managed by A. François.

1963—Company becomes Porcelaine Lafarge.

Klingenberg, Leonard, Dwenger, Blakeman & Henderson

Date Unknown—A. Klingenberg joins Kittel in china import business. Company becomes Kittel & Klingenberg.

1855—Peter H. Leonard joins firm. Company becomes Kittel, Klingenberg & Co.

1865—Leonard becomes a partner.

1866—Kittel retires. Company becomes Klingenberg & Leonard.

Latter Half of 1860s—C. Dwenger works as clerk for Klingenberg & Leonard.

1880—Partnership dissolved, and each partner continues business separately.

1894 and 1895—Klingenberg dies and C. Dwenger purchases Klingenberg import business and factory.

1898—Leonard firm goes into bankruptcy.

c. 1916—Company closes.

1898—Leonard, Blakeman & Henderson started by Leonard's son and previous Leonard employees.

1899—Leonard's son dies and firm becomes Blakeman & Henderson and only imports Limoges porcelain.

Date Unknown—Blakeman & Henderson closes.

Sazerat, Blondeau

1852—L. Sazerat starts manufacturing company with A. Margaine.

1853—A. Margaine leaves and joins P.J. Gibus.

1881—Sazerat starts partnership with P. Blondeau.

1891—Sazerat dies. Pichonnier and Duboucheron join Blondeau.

1906—T. Haviland buys company and turns it into a decorating studio.

Tharaud

1854-1884—Louis Tharaud operates factory in Limoges.

1920—Camille Tharaud re-opens factory.

1948—Goumot-Labesse, Tharaud's son-in-law, leaves company and starts his own decorating studio.

1956—C. Tharaud dies and his wife and children continue company.

1968—Company closes.

Vogt, Tressemanes & Vogt, Raynaud

1840s—J. Vogt starts New York company to import china.

1850s—Vogt starts exporting firm in Limoges.

1860s—Vogt starts decorating studio in Limoges.

Mid-1860s—Company becomes Vogt & Dose.

1870—Vogt's son, Gustave, takes over studio.

Early 1880s—E. Tressemanes starts partnership with Vogt. Company becomes Tressemanes & Vogt.

1891—Tressemanes & Vogt purchase two small manufacturing factories.

1907—Tressemanes retires and company named Porcelaine Gustave Vogt.

1910—M. Raynaud takes over Dwenger studio and starts decorating studio with his two brothers.

1919—Raynaud buys company and it becomes Raynaud & Cie.

1931—Business closes.

1952—Raynaud's son, André, takes over.

Raynaud & Cie is still in business.

Company Marks

AB (unidentified company)

AB porcelain mark 1.

AD (unidentified company)

c. early 1900's

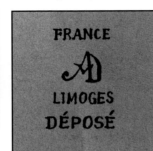

A&D decorating mark 1.

A&D (unidentified company, c. early 1990s)

1891+

A&D, decorating mark 1 in green or red.

Ahrenfeldt (c. 1859-1969)

1884-1891

Ahrenfeldt decorating mark 1 in red.

c.1891 to c.1896.

Ahrenfeldt decorating mark 2 in blue.

1894-c. 1896

Ahrenfeldt decorating mark 3 in green.

Ahrenfeld porcelain mark 4 in green.

c. 1896 and after

Ahrenfeldt porcelain mark 5 in green.

Ahrenfeldt decorating mark 6 in green or gold.

Ahrenfeldt porcelain mark 7 in green.

Ahrenfeldt decorating mark 8 in green.

Ahrenfeldt porcelain mark 9 in green.

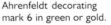

Ahrenfeldt porcelain mark 10 in green.

Ahrenfeldt porcelain mark 11 in green.

c. 1940s and after

Ahrenfeldt decorating mark 12 in blue

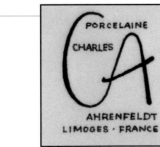

Ahrenfeldt decorating mark 13.

AJCO (unidentified company)

c. 1930s and after

AJCO decorating mark 1 in blue.

Alice & Charly (1995-present)

1995-c. 1999

Alice & Charly decorating mark 1 in black.

213

François Alluaud (1798-1876)

Aluminite René Frugier (1899-1964)

c. 1999-current

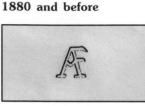

Alice & Charly decorating mark 2 in black.

1880 and before

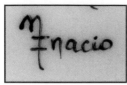

Alluaud porcelain mark 1, in blue on wares dated 1867 and impressed until 1880.

c. 1920s

Frugier porcelain mark 1.

1936+

Frugier porcelain mark 2.

c. 1950s

Frugier porcelain mark 3.

From 1964 (company now part of Haviland)

Frugier/Haviland porcelain mark 4.

Ancienne Manufacture Royale (1770-present, under many different names and ownership)

Before 1774 ————————————————————

Ancienne Manufacture Royale porcelain mark 1.

Ancienne Manufacture Royale porcelain mark 2.

Beginning in 1774 —

Ancienne Manufacture Royale porcelain mark 3.

Before 1784

Ancienne Manufacture Royale decorating mark 4.

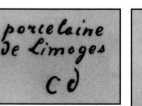

Ancienne Manufacture Royale mark 5.

After 1784 ————————

Ancienne Manufacture Royale mark 6.

Ancienne Manufacture Royale mark 7.

Ancienne Manufacture Royale mark 8.

(Société Porcelainière, 1929-c. 1986)

Used in 1929 ————————————————————

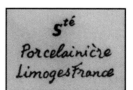

Ancienne Manufacture Royale porcelain mark 10.

Ancienne Manufacture Royale decorating mark 11.

Ancienne Manufacture Royale mark 9.

Mark registered in 1930

Ancienne Manufacture Royale decorating mark 12.

Ancienne Manufacture
Royale porcelain mark
13.

Ancienne Manufacture Royale decorating
mark 14.

Ancienne Manufacture Royale
decorating mark 15.

Ancienne Manufacture Royale
decorating mark 15 in gold.

Henri Ardant (1854-1878)

c. 1854

1858 and after

1865-

1869-

Ardant porcelain mark 1.

Ardant decorating
mark 2.

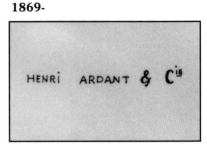

Ardant porcelain mark 3.

Ardant decorating mark 4.

Artoria (c. 1990s-present, formerly Manufacture Nouvelle de Porcelaine)

From c. 1990+ ————————————————————————————

Artoria porcelain mark 1 in
green.

Artoria decorating mark 2 in
black.

Artoria decorating mark 4 in
gold.

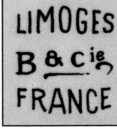

Artoria decorating mark 5 in black.

AV (unidentified company)

Bac & Perigault (c. 1875-1897)

Julien Balleroy & Cie

c. 1960

Balleroy Frères (1908- c. 1937)

c. 1908-c. 1937

AV porcelain mark 1 impressed,
possibly Aragon & Vultury.

Bac & Perigault porcelain
mark 1 in green.

Balleroy porcelain mark 1.

Balleroy Frères porcelain
mark 1.

Balleroy Frères decorating mark 2.

215

Barat (c. mid-1950s-c. mid-1970s, unidentified company)

Barat decorating mark 1 in green.

Barny & Rigoni (1894-1906)

1849-1902

Barny & Rigoni porcelain mark 1.

1902-1904

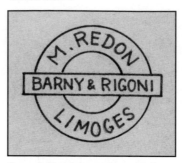

Barny & Rigoni decorating mark 2, also probably used later by La Porcelaine Limousine.

(& Langle)
1904-1906 ————

Barny & Rigoni porcelain mark 3 in green.

Bassett (before 1874-1963, U.S. importer)

Barny & Rigoni decorating mark 4.

c. 1890-1963

Bassett decorating mark 1 in red or green.

Bawo & Dotter/The Elite Works (1860s-1932)

c. 1860s-1870s ——

Bawo & Dotter decorating mark 1 in red.

Bawo & Dotter decorating mark 2 in red or green.

c. 1872-c. 1891

Bawo & Dotter decorating mark 3 in red.

c. 1891-1896 ————

Bawo & Dotter decorating mark 4 in red.

Bawo & Dotter decorating mark 5 in red.

c. 1891-1920

Bawo & Dotter decorating mark 10 in red.

1896-1920 ————

Bawo & Dotter porcelain mark 6 in green.

Bawo & Dotter decorating mark 7 in red.

Bawo & Dotter decorating mark 8 in red.

Bawo & Dotter porcelain mark 9 in green.

Bawo & Dotter porcelain mark 9.5 in green.

Bawo & Dotter porcelain mark 11 in green.

Bawo & Dotter decorating mark 12 in red.

1920-1932

Bawo & Dotter decorating mark 13 in red.

Bawo & Dotter decorating mark 14 in black and brown, with *Guérin, Pouyat, Elite Ltd.* printed inside emblem.

Beaux-Arts (unidentified company)

c. 1900

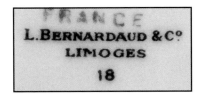

Beaux-Arts decorating mark 1 in green.

L. Bernardaud & Cie (1900-present)

1900-1929

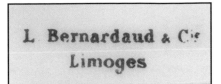

Bernardaud decorating mark 4 in red.

1900-c. 1942

Bernardaud porcelain mark 1 in green.

c. 1942-1978

Bernardaud porcelain mark 3 in green.

After 1929-1979+

Bernardaud decorating mark 5 in red.

Used in 1969

Bernardaud decorating mark 6 in red.

Current

Bernardaud mark 7 in green or gold.

Bernardaud mark 8 in green.

Beulé, Reboisson & Parot

Beulé porcelain mark 1.

B.H. (unidentified company)

1920s and earlier

B.H. porcelain mark 1 in green, possibly Blakeman & Henderson.

B.H. (unidentified company)

c. 1990s

B.H. decorating mark 2 in blue.

BK or KB (unidentified company)

Late 1800s to early 1900s

LIMOGES ∘ FRANCE ∘

Imperial

BK decorating mark 1 in red.

Blakeman & Henderson (1899-)

Blakeman & Henderson
Limoges- France

Blakeman & Henderson decorating mark 1 in green.

Blakeman & Henderson decorating mark 2 in red, green or gray.

Blanchard Frères

1890-1908

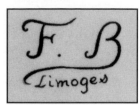

Blanchard decorating mark 1.

Blondeau, Pichonnier & Duboucheron (1891-1906)

1891 and after ──────────────

Blondeau porcelain mark 1 in green.

Blondeau decorating mark 2 in red.

Boisbertrand &Theilloud (1882-1902)/Boisbertrand & Dorat (1902-late 1930s)

c. 1929

Boisbertrand porcelain mark 1.

George Borgfeldt (1881-c. 1934, U.S. importer)

1900s-c. 1920 ──────────────

Borgfeldt decorating mark 0.5 in green.

Borgfeldt decorating mark 1 in green or blue.

After 1920

Borgfeldt decorating mark 2 in green.

Jean Boyer (c. 1919-1934)

1919-

J. Boyer decorating mark 1 in blue.

Georges Boyer (1934-present, Société Limousine de Porcelaine)

1919-1934

J. Boyer porcelain mark 2 in green.

1920-1934

J. Boyer decorating mark 3 in blue.

1934-1953

G. Boyer decorating mark 1.

1939-1962

G. Boyer decorating mark 2.

From 1953

G. Boyer decorating mark 3 in black or gold.

Used in 1979

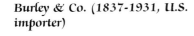

G. Boyer porcelain mark 4.

Broussaud

Used in 1979

Broussaud decorating mark 1.

B&T (unknown company, may be Boisbertrand & Theilloud)

Late 19th and early 20th centuries

B&T decorating mark 1.

Burley & Co. (1837-1931, U.S. importer)

1885-1931

Burley decorating mark 1 in red.

B.S. (unidentified company)

c. 1920s

B.S. decorating mark 1 in green.

CAR (unidentified company)

c. early 1900s

CAR decorating mark 1 in green.

CC (unidentified company, late 20th century)

CC decorating mark 1.

C.H. (unidentified company)

1920s+

C.H. porcelain mark 1 in green, possibly Bower & Dotter.

Chabrol Frères & Poirier (1917-1930s)

Used in 1929

Chabrol porcelain mark 1.

Chamart (1955-present)

Up to c. 1985

Chamart decorating mark 1 in black.

Late 1960s-current

Chamart decorating mark 2 in black.

Current

Chamart decorating mark 3 in black.

Chanille

c. 1990s-current

Chanille decorating mark 1.

Chapus & Ses Fils (1928-1933, Manufacture Porcelainière Limousine)

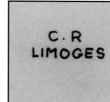

Chapus porcelain mark 1.

Chapus Frères (1933-)

Used in 1933 ———

Chapus decorating mark 2.

Chapus decorating mark 3.

Chapus porcelain mark 3.1 in green.

Chapus porcelain mark 4.

Chapus decorating mark 5.

Used by Raynaud beginning in 1974

Chapus/Raynaud porcelain mark 1.

Chastagner (1946-)

From 1950- ———

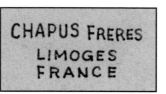

Chastagner porcelain mark 1.

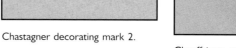

Chastagner decorating mark 2.

Chauffriasse & Rougerie (1926-1934)

Used in 1929 ———

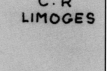

Chauffriasse porcelain mark 1.

Chauffriasse decorating mark 2.

C. et J. (unidentified company)

c. 1890s-c. 1920s

C. et J. decorating mark 1 in red.

CMC or GMC (unidentified company)

After 1891

CMC porcelain mark 1.

Coiffe Jeune (1887-1924)

Before 1891

Coiffe porcelain mark 1 in green.

After 1891

Coiffe porcelain mark 2 in green.

Comte d'Artois (unidentified company)

Coquet & Cie (1940-)

c. 1914-mid-1920s

c. mid-to-late 1900s

Before 1964

About 1964

Coiffe porcelain mark 3 in green.

Coiffe porcelain mark 4 in green.

d'Artois decorating mark 1 in blue.

Coquet decorating mark 0.5.

Coquet decorating mark 1.

Used in 1979

Henry Créange

Dadad (unidentified company)

R. Délinières & Cie (1860-1900)

c. 1907-1914

c. 1870s-1891

Coquet decorating mark 2.

Créange porcelain mark 1.

Dadat decorating mark 1, possibly the mark of Dadat et Chabrol, 1868-1872.

Délinières porcelain mark 1.

1891-1900

Délinières porcelain mark 1.1.

Délinières porcelain mark 2.

Délinières decorating mark 3 in red.

Délinières decorating mark 4 in red.

Demartial & Tallandier (1867-1883)

Gustave Demartial (1883-1893)

1867-1883

1883-1891

1891-1893

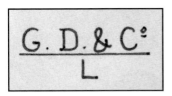

Demartial decorating mark 1.

G. D. & Cº
L

Demartial porcelain mark 1.1 in green.

AVENIR
FRANCE

Demartial porcelain mark 1.2 in green.

Demartial porcelain mark 2 in green.

Demartial decorating mark 3 in blue.

Depierrefiche (unidentified company)

c. 1920s-c. 1940s

Depierrefiche decorating mark I in red.

Descottes, Reboisson & Baranger

1933-1927

Descottes porcelain mark I.

Philippe Deshoulières

c. late 1990s-current

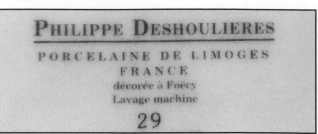

Deshoulières decorating mark I in black.

Florica Dragan

c. 1990s-current

Dragan decorating mark I in gold.

Dubarry (c. 1950s-present, English importer)

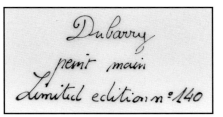

Dubarry decorating mark I in black.

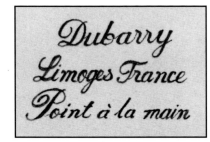

Dubarry decorating mark 2 in black.

Dubarry decorating mark 3 in gold.

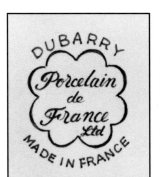

Dubarry decorating mark 4.

Dubarry decorating mark 5 in black.

L. Dubois (1915)

Dubois decorating mark I.

E.G.D. & Co. (unidentified company)

c. 1890s

E.G.D. & C. decorating mark 1 in green.

Eximious (c. early 1980s-present)

From 1982

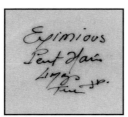

Eximious decorating mark 1 in black.

Fabergé (mid 1990s-present)

Late 1900s

Fabergé decorating mark 1 in gold.

F&F (unidentified company)

c. late 1900s

F&F mark 1

Flambeau China (L.D.B. & C., c. late 1890s-c. WW I)

Flambeau porcelain mark 1 in green.

Flambeau decorating mark 2 in red.

Flambeau decorating mark 3 in green.

Flambeau decorating mark 4 in green.

Flambeau decorating mark 5 in green, red or blue.

Flambeau decorating mark 6 in green.

Flambeau decorating mark 7 in green.

Florale (unidentified company)

c. 1920s

Florale decorating mark 1 in green.

Florence (unidentified company)

Used in 1979

Florence decorating mark 1.

Florence decorating mark 2 in black.

Fontanille & Marraud (1943-)

1943 and after

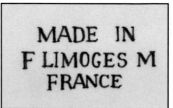

Fontanille decorating mark 1.

Fontanille decorating mark 2.

Fontanille decorating mark 2.1.

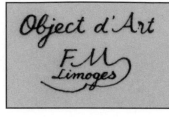

Fontanille decorating mark 3.

Fontanille porcelain mark 4.

André François (1919-1934)

French Accents (1983-present, importer)

Current

Fontanille decorating mark 5.

Fontanille decorating mark 6 in brown and gold.

François porcelain mark 1 in green.

French Accents decorating mark 1 in black.

French & Pacific Trading Corporation (La Gloriette)

Current

French & Pacific decorating mark 1 in black.

GC (unidentified company)

Late 1900s

GC decorating mark 1 in black.

GDF (unidentified company)

c. 1950

GDF decorating mark 1 in green and black.

Gérard, Dufraisseix & Morel (GDM, 1881-1890)

Gérard, Dufraisseix & Morel porcelain mark 1 in green.

Gérard, Dufraisseix & Morel decorating mark 2 in blue, black, gray, red or brown.

Gérard, Dufraisseix & Cie (1890-1900)

Gérard, Dufraisseix porcelain mark 1 in green.

Gérard, Dufraisseix decorating mark 2 in blue, black, gray, red or brown.

Gérard, Dufraisseix, Abbot (GDA, 1900-present)

c. 1900 —————— (Creation by Feure for Bing) ——————

Gérard, Dufraisseix, Abbot porcelain mark 1 in green.

Gérard, Dufraisseix, Abbot porcelain mark 2.

Gérard, Dufraisseix, Abbot decorating mark 3.

(Creation by Colonna for Bing)

Gérard, Dufraisseix, Abbot decorating mark 4

1900-1941 —————

Gérard, Dufraisseix, Abbot decorating mark 5 in red, purchased by Robert Haviland in 1941.

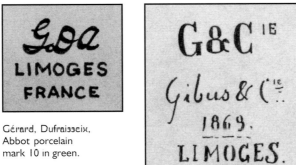

Gérard, Dufraisseix, Abbot decorating mark 5.1 in red.

1900-1953

Gérard, Dufraisseix, Abbot porcelain mark 6 in green.

1941-1976

Gérard, Dufraisseix, Abbot decorating mark 9.

From 1977

Gérard, Dufraisseix, Abbot decorating mark 7 in red or green.

c. 1980s+

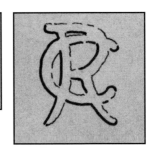

Gérard, Dufraisseix, Abbot porcelain mark 10 in green.

Gibus & Cie (1853-1872)

Gibus porcelain mark 1.

(with A. Margaine)

Gibus porcelain mark 2.

Gibus & Redon (1872-1881)

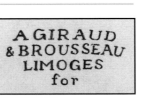

Gibus & Redon porcelain mark 1.

A Giraud (1920s-present)

1920s and used in 1979 —————

Giraud porcelain mark 1 in green.

Giraud porcelain mark 2 in green.

(with Brousseau)

1935-1967

Giraud decorating mark 3 in blue.

Used in 1979 —————

Giraud decorating mark 4.

Giraud decorating mark 4.1 in black.

After 1979

Giraud decorating mark 5.

Goumot-Labesse (1948-1979+)

1955-1977

Goumot-Labesse decorating mark 1.

From 1977

Goumot-Labesse decorating mark 2.

William Guérin (1836-1932)

From 1877

Guérin porcelain mark 0.1 impressed.

Guérin porcelain mark 0.2 in green.

Before 1891

Guérin porcelain mark 1 in green

Guérin porcelain mark 2 in green.

Guérin decorating mark 3 in red, rare.

1891-1932

Guérin porcelain mark 4 in green.

Guérin decorating mark 4.1 in green.

Guérin decorating mark 7 in blue or red.

Guérin decorating mark 5 in blue, gold, red, green or brown.

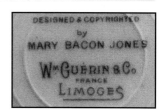

Guérin decorating mark 6 in blue.

Oscar Gutherz (After 1875-1883+)

Gutherz decorating mark 1 in red or blue.

Gutherz decorating mark 2 in red.

H&C (unidentified company)

Late 1800s

H&C porcelain mark 1, not a Haviland & Co. mark.

Haviland & Co.

Blank and Decorator Marks

HAVILAND & CIE. 1842-1931

BLANKS:

Mark A — *Incised on Tablet* — 1853

Mark B — HAVILAND H&Cº *Incised* — 1865

Underglaze Green Marks

Mark C — H&Cº — 1876-1879

Mark D — H&Cº — 1876-1886

Mark E — H&Cº — 1877

Mark F — H&Cº L — 1876-1889

Mark G — H&Cº DEPOSE — 1887

Mark H — H&Cº L FRANCE — 1888-1896

Mark I — Haviland France — 1894-1931

DECORATOR MARKS:

Varied Colors Overglaze

Mark a — FABRIQUÉ PAR HAVILAND & Cº POUR J.W. BOTELER & BRO. WASHINGTON / HAVILAND & Cº LIMOGES — prior to 1876

Mark b — H&C — 1876-1878

Mark c — HAVILAND & Cº Limoges — 1876-1878 / 1889-1931

Mark d — HAVILAND & Cº — 1879-1883

Mark e — H&Cº ELITE — 1878-1883

Mark f — H&Cº SPECIAL — 1879-1889

Mark g — HAVILAND LIMOGES — 1879-1889

Mark h — Haviland Limoges Feu de Four — 1893-1895

Mark i — Décoré par HAVILAND & Cº Limoges — 1905-1930 (America) 1926-1931 (France)

HAVILAND & Co. 1875-1885

Haviland Pottery and Stoneware

Mark V — H & Cº L — 1875-1882

Mark W — HAVILAND & Cº Limoges — 1875-1882

Mark X — H&Cº — 1883-1885

Mark Y — H & Cº L HAVILAND — 1883-1885

Haviland & Co. marks. Courtesy of Haviland Collectors Internationale Foundation and Wallace J. Tomasini, Ph.D.

Frank Haviland/Théodore Haviland

FRANK HAVILAND 1910-1931

BLANKS:

Mark A1 — FRANK HAVILAND LIMOGES — 1910-1914

Mark A2 — FRANK HAVILAND Limoges Limoges — 1914-1925

Mark A3 — FRANK HAVILAND L B S LIMOGES — 1925-1931

THÉODORE HAVILAND 1892-1967

BLANKS:

Colors Usually Green Underglaze

Mark J — TH — 1892

Mark K — PONT-MERY FRANCE — 1892

Mark L — néo Haviland Limoges France — 1893

Mark M — T & H — 1894-1957

Mark N — Blue — 1912

Mark O — — 1920-1936

Mark P — — 1936-1945

Mark Q — Haviland France — 1946-1962

Mark R — Haviland France Limoges — 1962

Mark S — THÉODORE HAVILAND NEW YORK *Green or Black* — 1936

Mark T — Théodore Haviland MADE IN AMERICA *Red or Black* — 1937-1956

Mark U — HAVILAND U.S.A. *Red* — 1957

DECORATOR MARKS:

Colors Green and/or Red Underglaze

Mark j — *Red* — probably 1892

Mark k — Porcelaine Mousseline Limoges FRANCE — 1894

Mark l — Porcelaine Mousseline Limoges FRANCE — 1894

Mark m — Porcelaine Theo. Haviland Limoges FRANCE — 1895

Mark n — Porcelaine Theo. Haviland Limoges FRANCE — 1895

Mark o — Théodore Haviland Limoges — 1897

Mark p — Théodore Haviland Limoges FRANCE — 1903

Mark q — Théodore Haviland Limoges FRANCE — 1903

Mark r — Théodore Haviland Limoges FRANCE — 1925

Mark s — HAVILAND LIMOGES FRANCE — 1958

Mark t — Haviland Limoges FRANCE — 1967

76

Frank Haviland and Théodore Haviland marks. Courtesy of Haviland Collectors Internationale Foundation and Wallace J. Tomasini, Ph.D.

Charles Field Haviland & Cie (1859-1881)

1881 and before

C. F. Haviland decorating mark 1 in black, brown or blue, also used later by GDM, GD, GDA and Robert Haviland.

c. 1865-1881

C.F. Haviland porcelain mark 2 impressed.

C.F. Haviland porcelain mark 3 in green.

C.F. Haviland porcelain mark 4 in black.

Frank Haviland (1910-1931)

1910-1914

F. Haviland decorating mark 1 in red.

1914-1925

F. Haviland decorating mark 2 in red.

1925-1931

F. Haviland decorating mark 3.

Robert Haviland (1924-present)

From 1924

R. Haviland porcelain mark 1 in green.

R. Haviland decorating mark 2.

1924-c. 1929

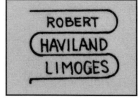

R. Haviland decorating mark 3.

(& Le Tanneur)
1929-1949

R. Haviland decorating mark 4 in brown.

From 1941-

R. Haviland decorating mark 5 in red.

R. Haviland decorating mark 5.1.

(& C. Parlon)
From 1949-

R. Haviland decorating mark 6.

Jammet & Seignolles (1950-)

Used in 1979

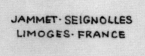

Jammet decorating mark 1.

J.B. (unidentified company)

Late 1900s

J.B., Mark 1, in brown. Porcelain mark.

J. McDaniel & Son (1880s-WW I, U.S. importer)

1880s-1890

JMcD&S decorating mark 1 in red.

c. 1891-WW I

JMcD&S decorating mark 2 in red.

A. Klingenberg (1880-1916)

1880s

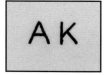

Klingenberg porcelain mark 1 in green.

Klingenberg decorating mark 2 in red.

1891-1894

Klingenberg porcelain mark 3 in green.

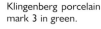

Klingenberg decorating mark 4 in red.

Klingenberg porcelain mark 5 in green.

(Dwenger takes over firm)

1895-1916

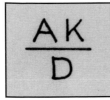

Klingenberg porcelain
mark 6 in green.

Klingenberg decorating
mark 7 in red.

Klingenberg porcelain mark
8 in green.

Klingenberg porcelain
mark 9 in green.

1775-1789

La Seynie decorating
mark 1.

Lafarge (1963-present)

1789-1797

La Seynie decorating
mark 2.

La Seynie decorating mark 3.

From 1963

Lafare porcelain mark 1.

Lafarge decorating mark
2.

From 1976

Lafarge decorating mark 3.

Lanternier (1857-present)

Before 1890

Lanternier decorating
mark 1 in blue.

Lanternier decorating mark 1.1
in blue or red

c. 1890

Langernier porcelain mark
2 in green.

Lanternier
porcelain mark 3 in
green.

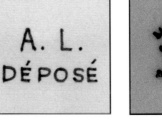

Lanternier decorating mark 4 in red.

Lanternier porcelain
mark 5 in green

Lanternier decorating mark 6
in blue, red or brown.

c. 1920s

Lanternier porcelain mark 6.1 impressed.

From 1914-current

Lanternier decorating mark 7 in red
and black.

Raymond Laporte (1883-1897)

1883-1897

Laporte porcelain mark 1.

Laporte porcelain mark 2..

1891-1897

Laporte mark 2.5.

Laporte decorating mark 3.

Latrille Frères (1899-1913)

1899-1913

Latrille porcelain mark 1 in green.

Latrille decorating mark 2 in red.

1908-1913

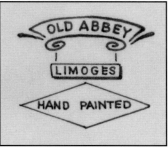

Latrille decorating mark 3 in green.

Latrille decorating mark 4 in black and red, may possibly be mark of H. Créange.

Laviolette (1896-1905)

Laviolette porcelain mark 1 in green.

Lazeyras, Rosenfeld & Lehman (1920s-c. 1930+, U.S. importer)

Lazeyras, Rosenfeld & Lehman decorating mark 1 in blue or red.

Lazeyras, Rosenfeld & Lehman decorating mark 1.5.

Lazeyras, Rosenfeld & Lehman decorating mark 2 in red.

Lazeyras, Rosenfeld & Lehman decorating mark 3 in green or gray.

L.B.H. (unidentified company)

c. 1890s

L.B.H. decorating mark 1 in red.

Le Tallec (1930-present)

1941-current

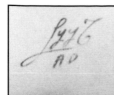

Le Tallec decorating mark 3 in blue.

DATE PRODUCTION CHART

A	B	C	D	E	F	G	H	I	J	K	L	M
1941	1941	1942	1942	1943	1943	1944	1944	1945	1945	1946	1946	1947

N	O	P	Q	R	S	T	U	V	W	X	Y	Z
1947	1948	1948	1949	1949	1950	1950	1951	1951	1952	1952	1953	1953

AA	BB	CC	DD	EE	FF	GG	HH	II	JJ	KK	LL	MM
1954	1954	1955	1955	1956	1956	1957	1957	1958	1958	1959	1959	1960

NN	OO	PP	QQ	RR	SS	TT	UU	VV	WW	XX	YY	ZZ
1960	1961	1961	1962	1962	1963	1963	1964	1964	1965	1965	1966	1966

α	β	γ	∫	ε	τ	η	θ	ι	χ	λ	μ	√
1967	1967	1968	1968	1969	1969	1970	1970	1971	1971	1972	1972	1973

∫	π	ɔ	S6	ϒ	υ	ч	χ	⊥	ω	RA	RB	RC
1973	1974	1974	1975	1975	1976	1976	1977	1977	1978	1978	1979	1979

RD	RE	RF	RG	RH	RI	RJ	RK	RL	RM	RN	RO	RP
1980	1980	1981	1981	1982	1982	1983	1983	1984	1984	1985	1985	1986

RQ	RR	RS	RT	RU	RV	RW	RX	RY	RZ	RRA	RRB	RRC
1986	1987	1987	1988	1988	1989	1989	1990	1990	1991	1991	1992	1993

RRD	RRE	DA	DB	DC	DD	DE	DF	DG	DH	DI	DJ	DK
1994	1995	1995	1996	1997	1998	1999	2000	2001	2002	2003	2004	2005

DL	DM	DN	DO	DP	DQ	DR	DS	DT	DU	DV	DW	DX
2006	2007	2008	2009	2010	2011	2012	2013	2014	2015	2016	2017	2018

DY	DZ
2019	2020

13 VILLA FAUCHEUR

67 RUE DE REUILLY

93–95 AVENUE DAUMESNIL

Le Tallec marks for production years, above line, from 1941-2020.

Leclair (1945-)

Used in 1979

Leclair porcelain mark 1.

F. Legrand & Cie (1904-1962+, with Betoule, c. 1910)

Used in 1919

Legrand porcelain mark 1 in green.

1923-1944

Legrand decorating mark 2.

P.H. Leonard (1880-1898, U.S. importer)

1880-1891

Leonard decorating mark 0.5 in red.

1891-1898

Leonard decorating mark 1 in red, blue or gray.

Lesme (c. 1852-c. 1881)

Lesme porcelain mark 1.

Lesme decorating mark 2.

Lesme porcelain mark 3.

Levy (late 1800s-early 1900s)

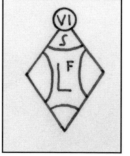

Levy decorating mark 1 in red.

Limoges, France (unidentified companies)

Before 1891

Limoges porcelain mark 0.5

c. 1891 and after

Limoges porcelain mark 1 in green, common to may manufacturers.

Limoges porcelain mark 2 in red.

Limoges porcelain mark 3 in green.

Limoges porcelain mark 5 in green.

Limoges porcelain mark 6 in green.

Limoges porcelain mark 7 in green.

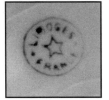

Limoges porcelain mark 8 in green.

Limoges porcelain mark 9 in green.

Limoges decorating mark 10.

Limoges decorating mark 11 in blue.

Limoges decorating mark 12 in red.

Limoges decorating mark 12.1 in red.

After 1908

Limoges decorating mark 13 in green.

Latter half of 1900s

Limoges decorating mark 15 in black.

Limoges decorating mark 16 in black.

Limoges porcelain mark 17 in green.

Limoges porcelain mark 18 in green.

Limoges decorating mark 19 in red.

Limoges mark 20.

Limoges porcelain mark 21 in green.

Limoges Art Porcelaine (unidentified company)

Limoges Castel (1944-)

Early 1900s

Limoges Art decorating mark 1 in green.

1944-1973

Castel decorating mark 1.

Used in 1950-1979+

Castel porcelain mark 2.

Castel decorating mark 3 in red, green or gold.

Used in 1979

Limoges Collectors Society (late 1990s-present)

Limoges Collectors decorating mark 1.

Limoges Collectors decorating mark 2.

Limoges Collectors decorating mark 3.

L.R. (unidentified company, possibly Lazeyras, Rosenfeld & Lehman)

c. 1920s

L.R. decorating mark 1 in red.

L.R.L. (unidentified company, possibly Lazeyras, Rosenfeld & Lehman)

c. 1920s

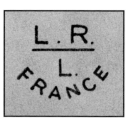

L.R.L. decorating mark 1 in blue.

Sigmund Maas (1894-c. 1930)

Maas porcelain mark 0.5 impressed, rare.

Maas decorating mark 1 in red, blue or green.

Madesclaire (until 1934)

Used in 1929

Madesclaire decorating mark 1.

Porcelaine Industrielle du Limousin

Used in 1979 and current

Manufacture de La Reine porcelain mark 1 in green.

Manufacture de La Reine (1840-present, Porcelaine Industrielle du Limousin)

Current

Manufacture de La Reine porcelain mark 2 in green.

Manufacture Nouvelle de Porcelaine (1960-1978+, became Artoria in 1990s)

Used in 1979

Nouvelle porcelain mark 1 in green.

Nouvelle decorating mark 2.

Charles Martin & Duché (1880s-1935)

After 1891

Martin porcelain mark 1 in green.

Martin porcelain mark 2.

Martin porcelain mark 2.1

Used in 1929

Martin porcelain mark 3.

Martin decorating mark 4 in green or blue.

P.M. de Mavaleix (1908-1914)

Mavaleix porcelain mark 1 in green.

P.M. de Mavaleix & Granger (1920-1938)

Mavaleix & Granger porcelain mark 1 in green.

Merigous

From 1978

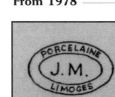

Merigous porcelain mark 1.

Merigous decorating mark 2.

P. Merlin-Lemas

Mid-1920s+

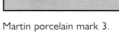

Merlin-Lemas porcelain mark 1.

Merlin-Lemas decorating mark 2.

L. Michelaud (1908-1962)

After 1918

Michelaud decorating mark 1 in blue.

Michelaud decorating mark 2 in blue.

234

Miautre, Raynaud & Cie (1929-1934)

Miautre porcelain mark 1.

S. Mounier (mid-1800s)

Mounier decorating mark 1 in red.

Nardon & Lafarge (1941-1963)

Nardon & Lafarge decorating mark 1.

Nardon & Lafarge decorating mark 2.

Other (illegible marks)

Other porcelain mark 1.

Other porcelain mark 2.

Pairpoint (U.S. decorator and importer)

c. 1880s

Pairpoint decorating mark 1.

Cesar Palma (1990s)

5/1000
Cesar Palma For HSN
Limoges France
Peint Main

Palma mark 1 in black.

L. Parant (1863-1868)

Parant porcelain mark 1 impressed.

Paroutaud Frères (1902-1916)

Paroutaud porcelain mark 1 in green.

Paroutaud decorating mark 2.

Paroutaud porcelain mark 3.

P. Pastaud (1920s-1950s)

Pastaud decorating mark 1 in gold.

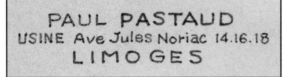

Pastaud mark 3.

Pastaud porcelain mark 2 in green.

A. Pillivuyt (1913-1936)

Used in 1929

Pillivuyt porcelain mark 1.

Pillivuyt decorating mark 2.

235

Pitkin & Brooks (1874-1917, U.S. importer)

1903-1917

Pitkin decorating mark 1 in purple or red.

Plainemaison Frères (1889-1909)

Mark registered in 1895

Plainemaison porcelain mark 1 in green.

Porcelaine Blanche

Used in 1929

Blanche decorating mark 1.

Porcelainierie de La Haute-Vienne (1920-1959)

Haute-Vienne porcelain mark 1.

Porcelaine Limousine (1906-1938)

Haute-Vienne decorating mark 2.

Porcelaine Limousine porcelain mark 1 in green.

Porcelaine Limousine decorating mark 2 in red, used earlier by Martial Redon & Cie.

Porcelaine Limousine decorating mark 2.1 in red.

Porcelaine Limousine porcelain mark 3 in green.

Porcelaine Limousine porcelain mark 4 in green.

Porcelaine Pallas

1927-1950

Pallas decorating mark 1.

Pouyat (1832-1932)

From 1851-c. 1876

Pouyat porcelain mark 1 in green.

Pouyat decorating mark 2 in red.

c. 1876-1890

Pouyat porcelain mark 3 in green.

Pouyat decorating mark 4 in red.

c. 1880s-c. 1890s

Pouyat decorating mark 5 in red.

c. 1890s

Pouyat decorating mark 6 in red.

1891-1932

Pouyat porcelain mark 7 in green.

Pouyat decorating mark in green or in green and pink.

André Prevot (1952-)

Used in 1979

Prevot decorating mark 1.

PU (unidentified company, 1st half of 20th century)

PU decorating mark 1 in orange.

Puy de Dôme

c. 1990's

Puy de Dôme mark 1.

Martial Raynaud & Cie (1910-1952)

1910-1919

Raynaud decorating mark 1.

1920s-1930s

Raynaud porcelain mark 2 in green.

Raynaud decorating mark 3 in purple.

André Raynaud (1952-present)

1952-1960

Raynaud porcelain mark 4.

Raynaud decorating mark 5.

Used in 1979

Raynaud porcelain mark 6.

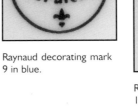

Raynaud decorating mark 7 in blue.

From 1960 and used in 1979

Raynaud porcelain mark 8.

Raynaud decorating mark 9 in blue.

Raynaud porcelain mark 10 in green.

Reboisson, Baranger et Cie (1927-1940)

Reboisson decorating mark 1.

Martial Redon & Cie (1882-1896)

c. 1882

Redon porcelain mark 0.5 in green.

Redon porcelain mark 0.6.

Redon decorating mark 1 in red.

1882-1890

Redon porcelain mark 2 impressed and in green.

1882-1896 ──────────────────

Redon decorating mark 3 in red, used later by La Porcelaine Limousine.

Redon decorating mark 4 in red.

1891-1896

Redon porcelain mark 5 in green.

c. 1990s-

Ribierre decorating mark 1 in black.

Riffaterre

c. 1900

Riffaterre decorating mark 1.

Robj (1921-1931, Paris retailer)

Robj decorating mark 1.

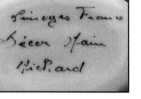

Robj decorating mark 2.

Rochard (1972-present)

Rochard decorating mark 1 in black.

Current

Rochard decorating mark 2 in black.

Rochard decorating mark 3 in black.

Rochard decorating mark 4 in black.

c. 1998-current

Rochard decorating mark 5 in black.

Rousset & Guillerot, 1924-1927; R. Guillerot and Dessagne, 1927-1936)

Rousset porcelain and decorating mark 1.

RP (unidentified company)

c. late 1900s

RP porcelain mark 1.

Royal (unidentified company)

Royal decorating mark 1 in green.

Royal China (unidentified company)

c. 1920s and after

Royal China decorating mark 1 in red.

Ruaud (1850s-1869)

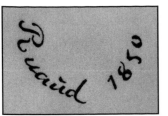

Ruaud porcelain mark 1.

L. Sazerat (1852-1891)

Sazerat porcelain mark 1 impressed and in green.

Sazerat porcelain mark 1.1 in green.

Sazerat decorating mark 2 in red.

Scotland's Yard Studio (U.S. decorator of Limoges boxes)

1990s

Scotland Yard's decorating mark 1.

S&D Limoges (1981-present)

1999-current

S&D decorating mark 1 in gold or black.

Serpaut (1923-1962)

1923-1930

Serpaut porcelain mark 1 in green.

After 1930

Serpaut decorating mark 2.

Siegel & Sohn (1906-1923)

1920-1923

Siegel porcelain mark 1.

Siegel decorating mark 2.

Sinclair (1996-present, importer)

Sinclair decorating mark 1.

Sinclair decorating mark 2.

Singer

1954-1974

Singer decorating mark 1.

Singer porcelain mark 2 impressed.

Singer decorating mark 3.

S&S (unidentified company, possibly Lazarus Straus & Sons)

c. late 1800s-early 1900s

S&S porcelain mark 1 in green.

Lazarus Straus & Sons *(1866-1924,
became Nathan Straus & Sons in
1924 and closed in 1930s)*

c. 1890s-c. mid-1920s

Lazarus Straus & Sons
decorating mark 1 in blue,
red, green or gray.

SW *(unidentified company)*

After 1891

SW decorating mark 1 in
red.

Jules Teissonnière *(1928-c. 1962)*

Used in 1929

Teissonnière decorating
mark 1.

Dates uncertain

Teissonnière decorating mark 2.

L. Téxeraud *(1923-1936)*

Used in 1929

Téxeraud decorating mark
1.

Téxeraud decorating
mark 2.

Téxeraud decorating
mark 3.

H. Thabard *(1932-c. 1950)*

Thabard decorating mark 1.

Camille Tharaud *(1920-1968)*

1920-1945

Tharaud porcelain mark 1
impressed.

Tharaud porcelain mark 1.1
impressed and in green or
blue.

Tharaud decorating mark 2 in blue.

Tharaud decorating mark 3.

After 1945

Tharaud mark 4 in
green, blue or gold.

G. Thirion *(unidentified company, Paris
decorating studio)*

mid-late 1900s

Thirion decorating mark
1 in blue or green.

240

Thomas (1954; became Porcelaine de La Rose in 1985)

Used in 1979

Thomas decorating mark 1.

Touze, Lemaitre & Blancher (1918-1939)

Touze porcelain mark 1.

Tressemanes & Vogt (early 1880s-1907)

Early 1880s-1891

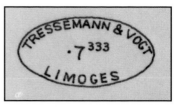

Tressemanes & Vogt decorating mark 1 in blue.

Tressemanes & Vogt decorating mark 1.1 in purple.

Tressemanes & Vogt decorating mark 2 in red, purple or gold.

Tressemanes & Vogt decorating mark 2.1 in blue.

Tressemanes & Vogt decorating mark 2.2 in blue.

c. 1891

Tressemanes & Vogt porcelain mark 3 in green.

1892-1907

Tressemanes & Vogt porcelain mark 4 in green.

Tressemanes & Vogt decorating mark 5 in red or gold.

Tressemanes & Vogt porcelain mark 6 in green.

Tressemanes & Vogt decorating mark 7 in red, purple, gold or brown.

Tressemanes & Vogt porcelain mark 8 in green.

Tressemanes & Vogt porcelain mark 8.1 in green.

Tressemanes & Vogt porcelain mark 9 in green.

Tressemanes & Vogt porcelain mark 10 in green.

Gustave Vogt (1907-1919)

Tressemanes & Vogt porcelain mark 11 in green.

Tressemanes & Vogt decorating mark 12 in purple or red.

241

Tressemanes & Vogt decorating mark 13 in purple.

Tressemanes & Vogt decorating mark 14 in green.

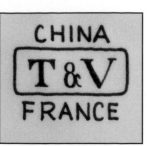

Tressemanes & Vogt decorating mark 15 in purple.

Turgot

Current

Union Céramique (1909-1938)

Tressemanes & Vogt decorating mark 16 in purple.

Tressemanes & Vogt decorating mark 17 in purple.

Turgot porcelain mark 1.

Union Céramique porcelain mark 1 in green.

Union Céramique decorating mark 2 in red.

Union Limousine (1908-present)

Prior to 1950   **1950-1975**

Used in 1979

Union Limousine porcelain mark 1.

Union Limousine porcelain mark 2.

Union Limousine porcelain mark 3.

Union Limousine porcelain mark 4.

Union Porcelainière (1928-1963)

1928-1940   **1928-1963**

VF (unidentified company, possibly Vultry Frères)

Early 1890s

Parry Vieille

Current

Union Porcelainière porcelain mark 1.

Union Porcelainière decorating mark 2.

VF decorating mark 1 in green.

Vieille decorating mark 1.

Vignaud (1911-1938)

1911-1938

Vignaud porcelain mark 1 in green.

Vignaud decorating mark 2.

Vignaud decorating mark 3.

1938-1970

Vignaud porcelain mark 4 in green.

Vignaud porcelain mark 5.

Villegoureix (1922-1929)   **Vultury Frères (1897-1904)**

Villegoureix mark 1.

Vultury porcelain mark 1 in green.

"Fake" Limoges Marks

The following marks are appearing more frequently on porcelain, but they are not marks of companies in Limoges, France. The first tip-off that these marks are "fake" is that although they appear relatively new, they do no include the word, *France*. The McKinley Tariff law of 1891 required that goods imported into the U.S. list the county of origin. As a result, nearly all porcelain from Limoges, France, imported since 1891 includes the word, *France*, in the mark. (Many of the Limoges, France, marks before 1891, however, do not include the word, *France*.)   Pieces with these "fake" marks probably originate from countries in Asia. Some of these "fake" marks are even now beginning to appear with the word, *France*, to indicate, falsely, that they originated in France. There is another fake mark, *Amoges*, which almost looks like *Limoges*; unfortunately, we were not able to obtain a photograph of it to include here. As the values of true Limoges porcelain continue to increase, more "fake" marks will most likely begin to appear.

"Fake" Limoges mark 1, probably from Taiwan.

"Fake" Limoges mark 2.

"Fake" Limoges mark 3, from the People's Republic of China (PRC).

"Fake" Limoges mark 4.

"Fake" Limoges mark 5.

"Fake" Limoges mark 6.

Contemporary Limoges Box Companies

We have provided below a brief description of the major companies that import/export, manufacture and/or decorate Limoges boxes. Most of the Limoges boxes on the market do not indicate the manufacturer or the decorator. At most they are marked over the glaze *peint main* or *peint à la mein* (hand painted) or *rehaussé main* (embellished by hand, but not entirely hand painted) and *Limoges France*. If the box is not marked *peint main* or *peint à la main*, the piece was probably not entirely painted by hand. Since most of the decorators of boxes in Limoges are individuals or small groups, they are not identified by the name of a company. Frequently, the boxes will be marked with the initials of the decorator, but there is no way to identify most of them. And, just because a box is marked as a limited edition, it does not mean that it is truly limited to a small number, say 500 or less. Furthermore, it usually means that a particular decoration is limited and not the blank itself.

The two most frequently seen porcelain marks are Artoria mark 1 and Manufacture de La Reine mark 1. Interestingly, Artoria only uses the porcelain mark on boxes they decorate with transfers and on blanks sold to other companies. Boxes decorated by Artoria that are entirely hand painted only have the Artoria decorating mark and not the porcelain mark.

The porcelain manufacturers sell their blanks all over the world, which means that many Limoges boxes are decorated by individuals and companies outside of France. Collectors looking for boxes decorated only in France will need to check the overglaze mark to make sure it includes the words *Limoges France* or just *France*. Additionally, because many companies and individuals sell "seconds," it is also important to look for the marks of the major importers/exporters, companies that generally sell higher quality boxes.

The companies that generally sell the best decorated boxes are Atelier Le Tallec, S&D Limoges, Chamart, Rochard, Artoria and Dubarry. All of the boxes sold by Atelier Le Tallec, S&D Limoges, Chamart and Artoria are entirely hand painted. Rochard and Dubarry also sell boxes decorated with transfers.

Below are company listings with brief descriptions:

Ancienne Manufacture Royale. In 1986 the company was purchased equally by Bernardaud and M. Denis Verspieren. There are relatively few boxes with this decorating mark.

Artoria. Previously called Manufacture Nouvelle de Porcelaine, the company was renamed Artoria in the mid-1990s. Pieces with the Artoria decorating mark are entirely hand painted. Artoria manufactures, decorates and exports their boxes all over the world. They have also obtained licenses to produce boxes from copyrighted materials, such as Disney and Peanuts characters. The current president of the company is Thierry de Merindol.

Chamart (Charles Martine). The founder of the company, Charles Martine, was the first person to begin importing Limoges boxes in the U.S. in the early 1950s, and his company was incorporated in 1955. Chamart is an importer, and all their boxes are entirely hand painted. Leny Davidson, the president of the company and the niece of the founder, states that about half of their porcelain blanks are exclusive to them. The company has a large showroom in New York.

Chanille. Chanille distributes boxes mostly to high-end retailers.

Dubarry. Headquartered in London, Dubarry distributes boxes all over the world, with their primary markets being England and the U.S. Dubarry distributes boxes from the French & Pacific Trading Company (La Gloriette) and other decorators in Limoges. While the majority of their boxes are hand painted, they do sell boxes that are decorated with transfers.

Eximious of London. Eximious has been importing Limoges boxes into the U.S. since 1986. Their boxes are sold primarily through their catalogue, *Eximious of London*. The company's boxes are marked *Eximious* and include boxes that are all hand painted as well as boxes that are decorated with transfers. Josephine Lewis is the president of the company.

Fontanille & Marraud. Fontanille & Marraud is a decorating studio in Limoges, which has been in business since the mid-1930s. All of the boxes that we have seen with the Fontanille & Marraud mark have been decorated with transfers and hand painted embellishments.

French Accents. This company distributes Limoges boxes in the U.S.

French & Pacific Trading Corporation. French & Pacific Trading Corporation, based in Chino, California, distributes Limoges boxes that are marked, *La Gloriette*.

GroundStrike. GroundStrike is a distributor of high end Limoges boxes. Started in 1997 and based in Texas, they sell boxes from Rochard, Artoria, Chamart and other importers. Their web site is www.groundstrike.com. The president of the company is Susan Juliano.

Le Tallec. Le Tallec is a decorating studio in Paris started in 1930 by the artist, Camille Le Tallec, who died in 1992. The company was subsequently purchased by Tiffany & Company in 1993. Using Limoges porcelain blanks, the company decorates boxes, dinnerware and giftware. All of their pieces are entirely hand painted. Tiffany has exclusive rights to 32 Le Tallec patterns, and the studio itself owns more than 350 patterns, many of which are interpretations of pieces from the 18th and 19th centuries. Production dates, beginning with 1941, are marked on the bottom of each piece, as noted in the chart in the section on marks. Pieces sold by Tiffany are also marked, *Tiffany & C° Private Stock*. Le Tallec is one of the finest porcelain decorating studios in the world. Their pieces are very expensive.

Limoges Castel. Limoges Castel, founded in 1944 in Limoges, is both a manufacturer and a decorator. Many of their pieces are decorated in blue with gold accents, and many are decorated with transfers.

Limoges Collectors Society. This company is a relatively new importer of Limoges boxes. They have a website: www.tolimoges.com. The president of the company is Atilda Alvarido.

Manufacture de La Reine. This is one of the oldest and largest porcelain manufacturers in Limoges.

McFarlin Limoges. A Texas based U.S. importer of Limoges boxes, which includes pieces decorated with transfers.

Puy de Dôme. This company is a Limoges box distributor.

Gérard Ribierre. Gérard Ribierre is a decorator located in Limoges.

Rochard. Rochard is one of the largest importers of Limoges boxes in the U.S. Based in New York City, Rochard was incorporated in the fall of 1972 and initially imported traditional dinnerware and giftware from Limoges. In 1974 Rochard began importing boxes; and along with Charles Martine (Chamart), introduced Limoges boxes in the U.S. The president of the company is Richard Sonking.

S&D Limoges. Based in Texas, S&D Limoges was founded in 1981 by Shirley Dickerson, who is president of the company. The company is known for designing unique, high quality boxes. Many of the blanks and decorations are specially designed by the company; and in addition, they are the sole U.S. distributor of boxes decorated by Alice and Charly, one of the finest porcelain decorators in Limoges. Beginning in 1999, the company began marking boxes that were designed exclusively for them. Two of the best designed and decorated boxes that we have seen are the company's small and large Imperial Court Monkeys, which are photographed in the section on S&D boxes. The company's website address is: www.sdlimoges.com

Scotland's Yard Studio. Mary Scotland is a U.S. decorator of Limoges boxes.

Sinclair Productions, Inc. Incorporated in 1996 and based in Florida, Sinclair imports Limoges boxes. The company offers a collectors club and has a website address: www.limogesboxclub.com. The president of the company is Hughes Longelin-Pingle.

Parry Vieille. Located in Limoges, Parry Vieille is one of the largest decorators of Limoges boxes. They produce many well decorated boxes that are distributed by Rochard, S&D Limoges and others. Most of their boxes are hand painted.

Bibliography

Auscher, E.S. *A History and Description of French Porcelain.* English translation and edited by William Burton. London: Cassell and Company, Ltd., 1905.

Blonston, Gary. "A Surprise in Every Box." *Arts & Antiques* (1995): 75-77.

Brega, Vanna. *Robj Paris: Le Ceramiche: 1921-1931.* Italy: Leonardo Periodici, 1995.

Cahiers de la Céramique du Verre et des Arts du Feu, No. 35 (1964).

Cameron, Elisabeth. *Encyclopedia of Pottery and Porcelain: 1800-1960.* New York: Facts on File Publications, 1986.

Carroll, Lewis. *Alice's Adventures in Wonderland.* Paintings by Angel Dominguez. New York: Artisan, 1996.

Celebrating 150 Years of Haviland China: 1842-1992. Written by Wallace J. Tomasini. Milwaukee, Wisconsin: Villa Terrace Decorative Arts Museum, 1992.

Chefs-d'Oeuvre de la Porcelaine de Limoges. Paris: Réunion des Musées Nationaux, 1996.

Child, Theodore. "Limoges and Its Industries." *Harper's New Monthly Magazine* 72 (1888): 651-664.

Cunynghame, Henry H. *European Enamels.* New York: G.P. Putnam's Sons, 1906.

Cushion, J.P. In collaboration with W.B. Honey. *Handbook of Pottery and Porcelain Marks.* 4th Edition. London: Faber and Faber, 1983.

d'Albis, Jean, and Céleste Romanet. *La Porcelaine de Limoges.* Paris: Sous le Vent, 1980.

Edouard Marcel Sandoz: de La Sculpture a La Porcelaine. Paris: Réunion des Musées Nationaux, 1999.

Enamels of Limoges: 1100-1350. New York: The Metropolitan Museum of Art, 1996.

Faÿ-Hallé, Antoinette and Barbara Mundt. *Porcelain of the Nineteenth Century.* English translation by Aileen Dawson. New York: Rizzoli International Publications, Inc., 1983.

Gaston, Mark Frank. *The Collector's Encyclopedia of Limoges Porcelain.* Paducah, Kentucky: Schroeder Publishing Co., Inc., 1980.

_____. *The Collector's Encyclopedia of Limoges Porcelain.* Second Edition. Paducah, Kentucky: Schroeder Publishing Co., Inc., 1994.

_____. *Haviland Collectables & Objects of Art.* Paducah, Kentucky: Schroeder Publishing Co., Inc., 1984.

Gérard (E.), Duffraisseix & Cie. *E. Gérard, Dufraisseix & Co, Manufacturers of the "Ch. Field Haviland" China, Limoges, France.* Reprint, N.p., n.d.

A Guide to Miniature Bottles. Berkeley, California: Cembura & Avery Publishers, 1972.

Harran, Jim and Susan. *Collectible Cups & Saucers.* Paducah, Kentucky: Schroeder Publishing Co., Inc., 1999.

_____. *Collectible Cups & Saucers: Book II.* Paducah, Kentucky: Schroeder Publishing Co., Inc., 2000.

Henderson, James D. *Bohemian Decorated Porcelain.* Atglen, Pennsylvania: Schiffer Publishing Ltd., 1999.

Kamm, Dorothy. *American Painted Porcelain.* Dubuque, Iowa: Antique Trader Books, 1999.

Klamkin, Marian. *White House China.* New York: Charles Scribner's Sons, 1972.

Klapthor, Margaret B. *Official White House China: 1789 to the Present.* Additions and revisions by Betty C. Monkman, William G. Allman, and Susan G. Detweiler. New York: Harry N. Abrams, Inc., 1999.

Kovel, Ralph M., and Terry H. Kovel. *Dictionary of Marks: Pottery and Porcelain.* New York: Crown Publishers, Inc., 1953.

_____. *Kovels' New Dictionary of Marks.* New York: Crown Publishers, Inc., 1986.

Landais, Hubert. *French Porcelain.* English translation by Isabel and Florence McHugh. New York: G.P. Putnam's Sons, 1961.

Limoges Porcelain Box: From Snuff to Sentiments (The). Text by Joanne Furio and photography by George Ross and Freddy Le Saux. New York: Lake Warren Press, 1998.

Loring, John. *Tiffany Taste.* Garden City, New York: Doubleday & Company, Inc., 1986.

Mannoni, Edith. *Porcelaine de Limoges.* Paris: Massin Editeur, n.d.

Masks. London: Prince's Trust Events Ltd., 1996.

Meslin-Perrier, Chantal. In collaboration with Lucile Monnerie. *La Manufacture de Porcelaine: Pouyat, 1835-1912.* Paris: Réunion des Musées Nationaux, 1994.

Millon, Joël, and Claude Robert. *Un Siécle de Luminaries: 1880-1980. Trés Belle Collection de Céramiques par Camille Tharaud. Art Nouveau-Art Deco.* Paris: Drouot Richelieu, 1995.

Segonds, Jean-Claude. *Les Créations en Porcelaine de Limoges: D'Édouard Marcel Sandoz.* Italy: Hermé, 1995.

Tardy. *Les Porcelaines Françaises.* Paris: Tardy, 1975.

Travis, Nora. *Evolution of Haviland China Design.* Atglen, Pennsylvania: Schiffer Publishing Ltd., 2000.

_____. *Haviland China: The Age of Elegance.* Atglen, Pennsylvania: Schiffer Publishing, Ltd., 1997.

Waller, Kim. "The Pure Porcelain of Limoges." *Town & Country* (April 1981): 203-209.

Waterbrook-Clyde, Keith and Thomas. *The Decorative Art of Limoges Porcelain and Boxes.* Atglen, Pennsylvania: Schiffer Publishing Ltd., 1999.

Wynter, Harriet. *An Introduction to European Porcelain.* New York: Thomas Y. Crowell Company, 1972.

Index

This is an index of manufacturing and decorating companies, retailers, artists (in italics), porcelain pieces by type and selected other key words. This index does not include page references to companies in the section on *Company Histories and Marks*, since the companies are already listed alphabetically in this section.